The Third Dimension:
Air Power in Combating the
Maoist Insurgency

The Third Dimension:
Air Power in Combating the
Maoist Insurgency

by

Gp Capt A K Agarwal

(Established 1870)

United Service Institution of India

New Delhi

Vij Books India Pvt Ltd

New Delhi (India)

Published by

Vij Books India Pvt Ltd
(Publishers, Distributors & Importers)
2/19, Ansari Road
Delhi – 110 002
Phones: 91-11-43596460, 91-11-47340674
Fax: 91-11-47340674
e-mail: vijbooks@rediffmail.com

CONTENTS

Foreword

The Maoist ideology in India owes its origins to the abject penury and stems from the all pervasive poverty in the country's hinterland. The Maoist insurgency is based on communist radical ideology based on the political ideas of Mao Tse Tung. This type of insurgency can be traced back to the 1946-51 Telangana struggle and later Naxal movement, started in Naxalbari – a tiny village in West Bengal – in the late 1960s which witnessed both active and dormant phases till the end of the 20th century. In the last one decade though, fuelled by the continuing exploitation of the peasants and poor tribals by the landlords and the mining/timber mafia, as well as neglect and corruption by the governmental offices; the Naxal/Maoist movement has moved from strength to strength covering more than 120 districts with the 'Red Corridor' stretching across the swath of forest lands from Andhra Pradesh in the south to Maharashtra, Chhattisgarh, Orissa, West Bengal, Jharkhand and Bihar and is expanding. The lack of socio-economic developments that have occurred in these regions from any governmental force is an issue the Naxalites have been able to exploit to the hilt in their calls for violent, Mao inspired, revolution.

Hitherto, the idea of Maoist revolution has been attracting a substantial section of the Indian society, which includes intelligentsia, literati and the academia. The thought of adivasis or the tribals and the oppressed and poor people rising in arms against great injustices caused by the merciless exploiters have had many sympathisers. The Indian cinema spearheaded by Bollywood has not only mirrored but also romanticised the issue with a slew of movies especially in the last four decades, some of which big box-office hits. Who would forget movies like Satyajit Ray's Pratidwandi (The Adversary) or Mirnal Sen's Calcutta 71 or Khwaja Ahmed Abbas's film 'The Naxalites' in the 1970s and the '80s. Recent films included Lal Salaam – Red Salute (2002), Hazaron Khwahishen Aisi (2005). The War Within (2010) raised the profile of Maoist movement and won many national and international awards. Last year Prakash Jha raised the bar further with his powerful and well-acclaimed film Chakravyuh when he dealt with the sensitive issue of the Maoist movement.

But, as it often happens in any society, the Naxal/Maoist movement has also undergone a transformation where the oppressed have turned into oppressors with the force of the gun. The Maoists may have a boastful agenda to take over the governance of the country through the force of arms, but, in reality, they have become the exploiters and extortionists. Today there is hardly any organisation in the dark portions of the 'Red Corridor' – whether public or private – which have not fallen prey to the Maoists extortionist tactics, because refusal would put the lives of the concerned officials/ managers at great risk with hardly a surety that they would, or could, be protected by the security forces. Actually, now a Ctach-22 type of situation has developed where the Maoists are not even allowing the works, related to genuine development initiatives by the government, to proceed without hindrance. Needless to say they are being aided and abetted by India's known adversarial neighbours who love to 'fish in troubled waters' in endless pursuit of their nefarious designs of bleeding India with a 'Thousand Cuts'.

While, the Indian government had woken up to the Maoist menace some time ago, with Prime Minister, Dr Manmohan Singh declaring it to be the biggest threat to the internal security of the country; the Central Government continued to term it as a 'Law and Order' issue, generally leaving it to the affected states to tackle the problem. But for some individual cases and that too somewhat temporarily, it is clear the policy has failed to produce the desired results. If the recent events are taken to be a yardstick, it is evident that Maoist violence has reached beyond all imaginable proportions. It took the merciless massacre of 29 Congress leaders and workers along with security personnel for the government to finally declare the Maoists as terrorists. In the meantime, Maoists continued to indulge in unabated violent acts, the latest being the June 13, 2013 indiscriminate attack on a train in Bihar killing three people.

The big question which needs to be asked is whether the latest acts of brutal violence have ended all notions of romanticism attached to the Maoist movement or not? If the answer to the above is in the affirmative then it is evident that action would need to be initiated in a concerted and unified manner by all the affected States, led by the Centre, to rid the country of this dangerously cancerous malady. But, how exactly could this be complex task be accomplished?

The author of this book, Group Captain A.K. Agarwal took a year plus long Sabbath from the IAF on a 'Study Leave' to join the USI as a Research Scholar to answer this very question. Even though the title of his book relates to the 'Third Dimension' i.e. 'Air Power in Combating the Maoist Insurgency', he has painstakingly researched the subject to bring out a comprehensive strategy to combat the Maoist menace in India.

The book is neatly arranged in eight chapters. Starting from the very definition of insurgency, the book chronicles and brings out lessons learnt from two insurgencies – the Algerian and the Malaysian – where airpower was used both in support as well as offensive roles. Bringing out the genesis of the movement, the Maoist Insurgency is covered in great detail in the following chapter. The author then goes on to explain the use of airpower in all its facets in combating the insurgency. This is followed by 'Legal Aspects' to bring out the 'pros and cons' of using airpower, especially, in an offensive role.

In the last chapter, the author has made recommendations on how to use airpower in combating the Maoist insurgency in India. In conclusion he observes that any counterinsurgency operation has to be based on a strong political will, aggressive anti-guerrilla tactics and, economic and social development of affected areas to win back the confidence of the people – a pre-requisite for which is to regain control of the insurgency affected areas. He opines that airpower is normally not employed as it is synonymous to destructive fire power and traditionally considered to be best utilised when fighting a foreign enemy and not citizens of the country. He therefore recommends use of airpower only in the support role to help defeat the insurgency in a shorter period with lesser loss of life and resources.

It is hoped that this eminently readable book will be of great interest equally to the planners/executioners for counterinsurgency operations as well as the students involved in the study of Maoist insurgency in India.

While one agrees that airpower should be used selectively while fighting the Maoist insurgency, there are a few counters to the established approach of not using airpower at all against a country's citizenry in the offensive role. First and foremost however, one has to define clearly as to what path the current insurgency is following. It is obvious that the present Maoist leadership has slid down many notches from an ideological armed struggle to that of downright thuggery and extortionist approach. In any case, there is no room for political reforms or for that matter, solving any other problem through violence in a vibrant democracy that India professes to be. On the other hand, if the Maoists have truly changed from being grand ideologues to lowly terrorists then they must be treated as such.

It is hoped the Central Governments will adopt its much prophesised 'all inclusive' policy to bring about the much needed development in the hitherto neglected areas, including the hinterland forest belts of India – an 'Iron Fist & a Velvet Glove' approach. While the velvet glove should be employed for accelerated development (sans the otherwise ever-pervading corruption), the Iron fist part could well include judicious use of airpower in selective offensive roles for quicker and decisive results.

Air Marshal (Retd) V.K. Bhatia

Introduction

Insurgencies are born out of long periods of social discontent, economic hardships and state apathy towards the neglected masses. This discontent can result in the oppressed population being motivated to support an insurgency professing utopia in the form of an appealing ideology which will be translated into good governance by the insurgents. In due course of time the affected areas experience violence against the state machinery. If the State continuous to neglect these backward expanses, it will realise one day, that these areas are no longer governed by the law of the land – but that the rule of the insurgent prevails.

The Maoist insurgency follows the well beaten path taken by most insurgencies. It was born out of the unalleviated indifference shown by States to its poor masses. This insurgency, motivated by the ideology professed by the Communists, is not a recent development. Its origin lies way back in 1947 during the Telangana struggle, initiated by the poor landless and oppressed farmers against the feudal landlords. It was nurtured through the violent efforts of the villagers of Naxalbari, a small village of West Bengal and today, it is in its prime. These poor agrarian workers and tribals, along with some educated ideologues, are greatly influenced by the ideology professed by Mao Tse Tung. The insurgents of today are aptly named Naxalites and are also known as Maoists. Yesterday's motley crowd of peasants are now organised on the lines of a regular army with an estimated strength of 8,000 to 12,000 cadres. As per the stated strategy of the Maoists, *"The Central task of the Indian revolution also is the seizure of political power. To accomplish this Central task, the Indian people will have to be organised in the people's army and will have to wipe out the armed forces of the counter-revolutionary Indian state through war and will have to establish, in its place, their own state."* Or in other words – the insurgents are at war with the country.

This insurgency should not be taken lightly. The influence of the Maoists has spread to 182 Districts of India and is concentrated in the States of Bihar, Jharkhand, Chattisgarh, Odisha and bordering Andhra Pradesh. The insurgents have a well-established intelligence set up, motivated revolutionary soldiers who are also sufficiently armed and trained. Their operations against the security forces are well planned and rehearsed before execution, which results in a high success rate for them. The icing on the cake for them is that they have the support of the poor people, who are the centre of gravity in any insurgency. The efforts taken by the insurgents have borne fruit and they are in control of large areas of central India which they call 'Liberated Areas'. In these areas, it is the rule of the Maoists, and not that of the Government of India, that reigns supreme.

The Central Government of India considers this insurgency to be merely a law and order problem and to be dealt with by individual states as a state subject. To assist the states, the Central Government has adopted a two-pronged strategy of security and development and created a new division called the 'Naxal Management Division' under the Ministry of Home Affairs. This Division is mandated with effectively tackling the Naxal insurgency from both the angles of security and development.

To ensure the success of development schemes and uplifting the insurgency affected areas, a pre-requisite would be a secure and peaceful environment conducive for such development work. For creating a secure environment, 74 battalions of Central Armed Police Forces (CAPFs) and Commando Battalions for Resolute Action (CoBRA) are employed in anti-naxal operations. The government is also planning to augment the existing CAPFs with 10,000 CRPF troops.

History tells us that air power has been used extensively to quell insurgencies. The British used air power in Malaya in 1945 while the French used it in Algeria in 1954. Even India employed offensive air power in Mizoram when the Mizo National Front (MNF) declared independence from the State of India.

The role of air power in such conflicts has been rather over-looked in favour of an army and police based focus. As per a study conducted by the Rand Corporation titled 'Air Power in the New Counterinsurgency Era', *"the role of airpower is downplayed, taken for granted, or simply ignored and it (air power) is usually the last thing that most military professionals think of when the topic of counterinsurgency is discussed."* The main factors that influence the use of airpower in insurgencies are political will, public acceptance of the need to use aircraft and the nature and strength of the insurgency. If air power is to be used in fighting an insurgency in a democratic state, the government must convince the people that it is not using excessive force, nor is it attacking civilians indiscriminately. The government will also be embarrassed if other States can claim that it is using excessive force. It is easy to mount a false propaganda campaign castigating the government for using aircraft against the insurgents.Airpower on its own cannot defeat an insurgency which has the support of the majority of the population. The use of offensive air power against such an insurgency will only cause great bloodshed and is counterproductive for the government.

Airpower when used in support roles in counterinsurgency operations results in greater flexibility and acts to the advantage of the security forces that are otherwise at a disadvantage as compared to the insurgents who enjoy the advantage of surprise and initiative. Airpower will not be able to eliminate the requirement of having ground forces deployed in counterinsurgency operations, it will definitely enhance the ground forces ability to gather intelligence and extend their reach.

In the recent past, air power was used to transport troops during the 26/11 attack in Mumbai. There is no doubt in any one's mind that air power in non-kinetic roles can play a vital role in containing any insurgency. Accordingly, air assets are being employed against the Maoists, albeit in a limited manner. The Cabinet Committee on Security, headed by the Prime Minister, has cleared the use of helicopters only for casualty evacuation, troop mobility and other logistic roles. Helicopters have not been permitted to be used in the offensive role, though return fire in self-defence has been authorised. The availability of air assets employed in support of the security forces has been limited for various reasons. Apart from manned aircraft, UAVs have also been pressed into action for intelligence gathering.

Satellite imagery is also being studied to identify areas which are cultivated by the Maoists for Opium, which helps in financing the insurgency.Intelligence inputs are vital for thwarting the designs of the insurgents. UAVs provide a method of mounting continuous and unobtrusive surveillance.

This book is organised in two parts. The first part describes the characteristics of an insurgency and then brings out how air power was employed during the Malayan Insurgency and the Algerian Emergency. From these two case studies, air power lessons are gleaned. Part II examines the Maoist Insurgency and thereafter brings out the roles in which air power is being employed in subduing this insurgency, and then suggests roles in which it can also be employed. Problem areas in the current employment of air power have also been examined. After touching on legal issues related to the use of air power in insurgencies, the study makes recommendations for consideration.

On Insurgencies

Insurgency Defined

An insurgency, as defined by the Indian Army Doctrine 2004 is - "an organised armed struggle by a section of the local population against the State, usually with foreign support."[1] Another definition given by the Central Intelligence Agency of USA is, "a protracted political – military activity directed towards completely or partially controlling the resources of a country through the use of irregular military forces and illegal political organisations."[2] The US Army Field Manual on Counterinsurgency Operations defines insurgencies as, "an organised movement aimed at the overthrow of a constituted government through use of subversion and armed conflict." When we study these definitions we see that the common areas are that insurgencies are organised struggles, with the existence of violence and the assistance of a foreign hand. It can be analysed that the final aim of an insurgency is to overthrow the government.

An Insurgency, at times, may have limited goals. For example, an insurgency may intend to break away from government control and establish a self-governing state within established ethnic or religious boundaries. The insurgency could also be aimed at solely obtaining stated political concessions which may not be attainable by peaceful means.

An insurgency is a kind of a civil war, where citizens of the same country fight against each other. However, a distinctive feature in a civil war would be that the two warring factions, at some point of time, are in control of a certain portion of the armed forces and territory. A classic example of this is the American Civil War (1861 – 1865).

An insurgency is an audacious act against the political and military might of a state. History of past insurgencies shows that this is possible. Insurgences generally follow a revolutionary doctrine and use armed force as an instrument of policy. However, an insurgency is different from a revolution in that revolutions are mass movements in which leaders appear subsequently. An insurgency is also different from a 'coup d'état'. A coup does not have mass participation and it is clandestine in nature in which the leadership of the state is overthrown by a small group, normally from the armed forces.

Insurgencies are also different from conventional wars. In conventional wars, the opponents are well prepared and trained. War is declared and on achieving political objectives, a cease fire is declared. Military power is an instrument of political intent and any war is characterised by fire power, and achieving an early victory is usually the goal. On the other hand, in an insurgency, the insurgent is not well equipped or trained in the initial phases. Only after the passage of a considerable amount of time can the insurgents build up sufficient political ideology and support for it. They are not interested in an early victory but their struggle is protracted in nature. Some examples of such protracted political and violent struggles are China (1927 -1949), Malaya (1948-1960) and Algeria (1954-1962).

Counterinsurgency Defined

Counterinsurgency on the other hand, is those actions taken by the government to defeat the insurgency. These actions will be all-encompassing and include security, economic, social, psychological and political efforts. The government would need to respond to the insurgents' violent actions by providing security to the people, enhancing its legitimacy in the eyes of the affected population and slowly winning the confidence and support of the people and severing their support to the insurgent.

Dr David John Kilcullen, a leading theorist on counterinsurgency, has professed a model for counterinsurgency. The model is structured as a *base*, viz. Information, *three pillars*, viz. Security, Political and Economic measures and a *roof*, viz. Control[3]. Information, the base, is the foundation for all other activities. This is because information helps in providing data on the situation and assisting the government in formulating a plan of action for creating stability and controlling the insurgency. The three pillars - security, political and economic measures must be integrated with the help of information. Information operations would include gathering, analysing and dissemination of intelligence; manipulating the media for assisting in counterinsurgency operations; and actions which adversely affect the insurgents' motivation and ideology. Information operations would also indicate the effects of the counterinsurgency operations on the population. Until an information base is developed, the three pillars of counterinsurgency cannot be effective.

The three pillars of security, political and economic actions rest on the base of information. These pillars have to be developed parallel to each other; otherwise the structure would be lopsided. We cannot have economic development without security. On the other hand, excessive security without adequate political and economic activity would be oppressive to the population and be counter-productive.

While building on each pillar, progress is determined by gauging the effectiveness of each action and the degree to which the population accepts the government's actions to be in their interest.

The security pillar is made up of para-military, police and military forces which will protect the population from the insurgents. The political pillar focuses on mobilising support for the government and marginalising the insurgents. The government would be required to make efforts to mobilise stakeholders in their support, extend governance and further the rule of law. A key element is the building of institutional capacity in all agencies of the government and Non-Government Organisations, and social re-integration efforts such as the disarming, demobilisation and reintegration of insurgents into civil society. These pillars support the roof of control. This is achieved by ensuring stability. Stability is sought as a means to an end; a step on the way to regaining control over an out-of-control environment.

Characteristics of an Insurgency

Insurgencies are Political Struggles. Theoretically, all wars are fought for a political purpose. Clausewitz has described war as an apolitical instrument, a continuation of political intercourse, carried on with other means.[4] In a conventional war, military action takes over once the political intent has been made clear. The government may modify the political intent throughout the war, but the military remains the main instrument of war. Insurgencies begin because of a state's inability to meet the people's basic needs. In an insurgency, the aim of both the insurgent and the government is to win the support of the population. [5] Therefore, politics plays a continuous role in an insurgency. An Insurgency is neither an arbitrary nor an indiscriminate political violence. It is a directed and focused political violence. Insurgencies cannot be resolved by the sole application of military force. The importance of the insurgent political infrastructure is mirrored in the comparatively diminished importance of insurgent military forces. Ho Chi Minh[6], in a note, giving instructions on the importance of politics, stated, "Politics is more important than military affairs." [7] There is no doubt that insurgent military actions play a primary role in an insurgency. However, the success of the insurgents on the battlefield is not crucial to the success of the insurgent movement. Insurgent forces can lose virtually every battle and still win the war. The Algerian insurgency was lost on the battlefield. But the insurgents won by political and diplomatic means.[8] On the other hand, the government can lose, if its forces lose on the battlefield.

One of the first steps towards an insurgency is establishing a political setup or political party. The party must have a leadership and most importantly, an ideology. Leadership provides vision, direction, guidance, coordination, and organisational harmony. The leaders of the insurgency will endeavour to educate the people regarding the 'cause' through propaganda. They must gain popular support. Their key tasks are to break the ties between the people and the government, attract them towards the insurgency and establish its credibility. They must replace the government's legitimacy with that of their own. The insurgent leaders must have a program that explains what is wrong with society and justify their actions against the state.They must promise great improvement after the government is overthrown. The leaders accomplish this through ideology. Ideology guides the insurgents in offering society a goal. The insurgents often express this goal in simple terms for ease of understanding by the common man. The ideology professed by the insurgent leaders will provide an overview of the perceived social inequalities and also provide justifications for the use of violence. The insurgency's future plans must be vague enough for broad appeal and specific enough to address important issues.

The source of the insurgency's strength is its political infrastructure. The rebel political infrastructure feeds on the perceived grievances that lead to the birth of the insurgent movement. Moreover, if the infrastructure is well constructed (e.g., small cells with limited knowledge of other cells), the government will have great difficulty in rooting out and destroying the infrastructure by non-military means. This infrastructure is very important for the insurgency to emerge victorious. The political infrastructure performs the under mentioned tasks vital to the survival, growth, and eventual success of the insurgency:

- Intelligence.
- Logistic and financial support
- Recruitment
- Political expansion.
- Sabotage, terrorism, and intimidation
- Establishment of a shadow government.

Intelligence. To be effective, it is important for the insurgent movement to be able to understand the capabilities and future plans of the government. This would include strengths and weaknesses of the political leaders and force composition of security forces. Accurate and timely intelligence is important in assisting the insurgents in planning their subsequent strategy and tactics, both militarily and politically. The local population is the best source for providing information regarding the build-up and deployment of government security forces. People, sympathetic to the insurgency in government organisations, are able to provide this important information. Locals, who are not in government organisations, are also able to assist the insurgents with significant information observing government troop movements or reporting unguarded conversation of government officials overheard in social or business settings.

Logistic Support. Insurgent sympathisers provide the insurgent forces with essential supplies of food and clothing that are readily available within the society. They can also obtain simple Off the Counter medicines such as pain killers, antiseptic solutions, dressing material etc. without arousing suspicion. Weapons are obtained from foreign sources or captured from the security forces.

Financial Support. Availability of funds is critical to any insurgency. It is used to buy weapons, write political propaganda, pay the insurgents and fulfil a number of needs. Financial support is obtained from locals sympathetic to the insurgency, extorted[9] or may also be collected from industrial houses as protection money.[10] Most insurgencies occur in impoverished areas. Therefore, the insurgents have to look for funds from abroad. Funds are obtained from diaspora sympathetic to the insurgency. As quoted in a study conducted by the Rand Corporation, "The LTTE ran a sophisticated international revenue generating operation that drew heavily on the diaspora which contributed at least $50 million a year." [11]

Recruitment. Essential to the growth of the insurgency, is the ability of the insurgent leaders to convert people to be sympathetic to their 'cause'. This enables the insurgent infrastructure to tap into a larger manpower pool from which to draw recruits as soldiers of the insurgency. This makes it possible for the insurgent forces to grow in strength even after suffering heavy casualties at the hands of the government security forces. To defeat the growing strength of the insurgents, if the government's strategy is to try and defeat the insurgency by concentrating its major effort using force, it would be counter-productive. Greater number of locals would be influenced by the 'cause' and disenchanted by the government's use of force. This would provide the insurgents' infrastructure, the opportunity to grow unimpeded; thus aggravating the government's military problem.

Political Expansion. For an insurgency to succeed or flourish, the leaders would have to put the insurgency onto a strong political footing. Small groups would need to be amalgamated within a bigger organisation.

Terrorism Sabotage and Intimidation.   With an aim to achieve publicity for the insurgency movement and it's 'cause', the insurgents resort to indiscriminate terrorism, sabotage of government installations and intimidation of the public. Another aim of terrorism and intimidation is to ensure that the population stops co-operating with government officials, and government security forces are tied down in combating terrorism instead of fighting the insurgents. Further, acts of terrorism bring forth repressive actions from the government against the local population. This facilitates in creating hatred for the government and sympathy towards the insurgent movement. During the Algerian insurgency, the ALN political branch carried out assassinations of important personalities, while the military branch of the ALN carried out indiscriminate terrorism in the cities. The repressive measures used by the French government helped in alienating the local population from the French, who were in power. [12] The terror campaign was so successful that the Muslim population became pro FLN and was ready to support the ALN in the insurgency without being coerced with the use of terror tactics. [13]

Establishment of a Shadow Government. Finally, the insurgent infrastructure can institute its own government, opposing the authority of the legitimate government in power. This is an effective strategy if certain geographic areas are effectively under the control of the insurgents. A shadow government challenges the acceptability and validity of the government by virtue of its announced political program, its control in certain areas, and its resoluteness in spite of attempts by the government in power to destroy the insurgency. The 'Jan Adalats' by the Maoist insurgents in areas controlled by them is another example of this.

Insurgencies are People Centric. Fundamental to an insurgency's strength and key to its survival and progression is the indistinct political infrastructure deeply entrenched in and spread through the general population. In an insurgency, there will always be an active minority supporting the insurgents, a passive majority which needs to be won over by both the insurgent and the government and an active minority opposing the insurgency. [14] 70 to 80 per cent of the population is neutral, while 5-15 per cent are active or hostile towards the insurgency. [15]

Without some support from the people, or at least their neutrality, the insurgency's infrastructure would be quickly endangered and eliminated. Without an infrastructure, the insurgency has no political arm; it is deprived of an intelligence apparatus, basic source of military manpower and logistical support. At the same time, the government's power also ultimately depends upon the support and loyalty of the general population. In the long run, no government can survive without the consensus of the people--least of all a government actively opposed by an appealing and aggressive insurgent movement. The centre of gravity for each side in an insurgency is located within the general population. For the insurgents the support of the active minority is required to favourably influence the neutral minority and win over it for its active and tacit supporters. For the government, it is the support from the people and acceptance of its legitimacy[16]; whoever wins over this centre of gravity, wins the battle. Political power flows from the people. During the Malayan Emergency, the strength of the communist guerrillas was estimated to be 10,000 and the strength of the Chinese villagers who were supporting the insurgency was around 50,000. In the words of Colonel RL Clutterbuck, "This is the real strength of the guerrilla movement. To get these 50,000 villagers to withdraw their support was the real point, not just to kill the 10,000 guerrillas." [17]

Insurgencies are Protracted in Nature. The insurgency in China lasted for about twenty two years. The Malayan and Algerian insurgencies went on for twelve and eight years respectively. It takes time for any insurgency to mature from the time the leaders organise an initial small movement, refine its political ideology, train the insurgents and win the support of the people and subsequently blossom the insurgency into an armed struggle. Insurgents would naturally find it difficult to overthrow the legitimate government and achieve a quick victory. The protracted nature of the insurgency acts as a double edged weapon. On one side, time permits the insurgency to strengthen its movement, gaining momentum, popular support and military strength. On the other hand, as time keeps passing with an active insurgency, it tends to weaken and discredit the government's ability to govern effectively and maintain law and order. Each day that passes with the insurgency in the lap of the government, it tends to add legitimacy and creates an air of certainty amongst the affected population on the subsequent victory of the insurgency. A protracted insurgency weakens the government economically. For example, the protracted nature of insurgency in Jammu and Kashmir has adversely affected tourism causing the state to lose a lot of money. As quoted by Ho Chi Minh, "Time is the condition to be won to defeat the enemy. In military affairs time is of prime importance. Time ranks first among the three factors necessary for victory, coming before terrain and support of the people. Only with time can we defeat the enemy."[18]

Mao Tse Tung, considered by many to be the godfather of modern insurgent warfare theory, promoted the concept of a protracted, three-phased conflict. Mao's concept began with the establishment of secure base areas and the creation of a political infrastructure; progressed through guerrilla attacks on the government and actions to build popular support, culminated in a more conventional war seeking quick and decisive victory. Based on his experiences in China, Mao knew such a struggle could continue for years if not decades. His concept included the flexibility to move from one phase to another in either direction depending upon the situation at hand.[19] Quick victory was not important because time and the continuing insurgency would, in Mao's view, eventually bring victory to the rebel cause.

Insurgencies are not Costly for the Insurgent. One of the main objectives of the insurgent is to undermine the authority of the government and create disorder. Creating disorder is not costly or difficult. For example, if the insurgent blows up a road - not a very difficult and expensive task - the government will be forced to protect all roads in the area from a similar fate. It would have to invest a considerable amount of resources in terms of security forces for this task. The very threat of insurgency disrupts progress and growth for the government in the affected areas. The government is duty bound to maintain law and order, ensure progress and prosperity of the state. Therefore, when we compare the cost of waging an insurgency to the cost of fighting it, we see that the government spends much more than the insurgent. This is another reason why insurgencies can be protracted in nature. The cost of waging it is acceptable to the insurgent.

Insurgencies Have External Support. As brought out in the definition of an insurgency, there is a factor of external support. External support can give an insurgency moral, political, technical financial and military support. In the initial phases of the insurgency, external support is not very important. It would be difficult for the insurgent to utilise military support till the insurgency has developed to a certain stage of maturity. The insurgents can obtain arms and ammunition from raids on security forces. Once the insurgency matures and moves on to a higher level of warfare, external support becomes very critical for its victory. For example, during the Algerian insurgency, the borders along Tunisia and Morocco were sealed. This prevented the supply of arms to the ALN resulting in the defeat of the insurgents. There are three types of external support:

- State Sponsored.

- Diaspora sponsored.

- Other Non-State Actors sponsored.

State Sponsored. Foreign governments support insurgencies as an instrument to increase their regional influence. For example Pakistan supports insurgency in Afghanistan in order to increase its influence along its borders. States may also use insurgencies to effectively destabilise neighbouring countries. Internal stability and security is one of the most important agendas for any government. Considerable money and resources are expended in controlling any insurgency. India maintains a very high level of troops and para-military forces in Jammu and Kashmir to battle the on-going insurgency. As per the Annual Report Ministry of Home Affairs, 2010-2011, towards the Security Related Expenditure (SRE) scheme, assistance is provided to effected states for recurring expenditure relating to insurance, training and operational needs of security forces. Rs 60 crore were released during 2009-10 under this scheme. Rs 580 crore was provisioned for this scheme for 2010-11. In addition, 73 battalions of Central Para Military Forces (CPMFs) are deployed for assisting the State Police in fighting the Maoist insurgents in States of Andhra Pradesh, Bihar, Chhattisgarh, Jharkhand, Madhya Pradesh, Maharashtra, Orissa, Uttar Pradesh and West Bengal.

Diaspora Sponsored. Diaspora or the immigrant community living in other countries can also support insurgencies in their countries. These communities can fund insurgencies with large amounts of money or arm the insurgents. Their support can significantly increase the insurgent's capabilities and ability of the insurgency to succeed in countering the government's response. The LTTE successfully exploited the Tamilian diaspora in foreign countries for financing the insurgency in Sri Lanka.

Other Non-State Actors. Support to insurgencies may also come from other non-state actors such as religious groups, revolutionary groups, wealthy individuals and human rights organisations. Support from these non-state actors helps in strengthening the insurgency in the initial period. [20]

Insurgencies are Unconventional / Guerrilla Wars. As defined by the Indian Armed Forces Joint Doctrine on Sub-Conventional Warfare insurgencies are included in sub conventional threats. The armed forces undertake sub conventional warfare against them, or, unconventional warfare – a matter of semantics.

The ultimate aim of any insurgency on the road to success would be to create a regular army to be able to defeat the government security forces. This will be achieved progressively. Till this is possible, the insurgents will follow one of Mao Tse Tung's principles of preserving oneself and destroying the enemy by resorting to guerrilla tactics by small units.[21] Guerrilla tactics are the classical asymmetric strategy employed by the weak against the strong. All successful insurgencies employ such tactics against stronger government security forces.

Guerrilla tactics are planned to avoid a decisive defeat at the hands of a stronger enemy. Although conventional forces are constructed around the mobility of large units, guerrilla forces base their operations on the mobility of the individual soldier. Operating in small units, guerrillas avoid presenting themselves as tempting targets to government security forces, which usually have vastly superior firepower at their disposal. Guerrillas fight only when it is to their advantage to fight, aiming to achieve minor victories to achieve major objectives. [22]

There are many benefits of guerrilla warfare. The insurgents' military actions divert the attention of the government away from the activities of the insurgent political infrastructure enabling it to propagate with minimal opposition. Guerrilla actions harass, dishearten, and embarrass the government. Successful guerrilla attacks can provoke harsh reprisals from the government. Although reprisals can take a heavy toll on insurgents, they always extract a heavy price in blood from the neutral population. These reprisals are usually counterproductive as they further facilitate in alienating the population from the government.

As a corollary to this, successful insurgent guerrilla tactics can achieve several positive results for the insurgents. The local population may choose to support the insurgents or take a neutral stance because the government is unable to protect itself or the people. Government security forces may experience fatigue and war weariness as the struggle becomes more protracted and the government seems not to be making any headway against the guerrilla forces. Government security troops may desert while insurgent forces gain in strength. This compounds the government's problem. Eventually, the correlation of forces may change in favour of the insurgents.

Endnotes

1.   Indian Army Doctrine.Headquarters Army Training Command Shimla.p 16.

2.   Guide to the Analysis of Insurgencies. http://www.fas.org/blog/secrecy/2009/02/ analysis_of_insurgency.html. Assessed on 28 November 2011.

3.   Kilcullen David J. Dr. Three Pillars of Counterinsurgency. http://www.au.af. mil/au/awc/awcgate/uscoin/3pillars_of_counterinsurgency.pdf. Assessed on 30 Nov 11.

4.   Clausewitz Von Carl. On War, Translated by Howard Michal and Paret Peter. Princetown University Press. p-87.

5.   Galula David: Counterinsurgency Warfare Theory and Practice. Pentagon Press A-38 HauzKhas New Delhi.   p 5.

6.   Hồ Chí Minh (19 May 1890 – 2 September 1969) was a Vietnamese communist revolutionary leader who was prime minister (1945–1955) and president (1945–1969) of the Democratic Republic of Vietnam (North Vietnam). He

was a key figure in the foundation of the Democratic Republic of Vietnam in 1945, as well as the People's Army of Vietnam (PAVN) and the ViệtCộng (NLF or VC) during the Vietnam War.http://en.wikipedia.org/wiki/Ho_Chi_Minh. Assessed on 09 January 2013.

7.   Pike Douglas: PAVN: People's Army of Vietnam, Novato: Presidio 1986. p-31.

8.   O'Ballance Edgar: The Algerian Insurrection. Faber and Faber, London. p 220.

9.   DNA 14 December 2010. http://www.dnaindia.com/india/report_red-rebels-get-richer-by-rs2500-crore-in-west-bengal_1480928

10. The Hindu. 11 September 2011. http://www.thehindu.com/news/states/other-states/article2442658.ece

11. Byman Daniel, Chalk Peter, Hoffman Bruce, Rosenaun William & Brannan David: Trends in Outside Support for Insurgent Movements, Rand Corporation, Santa Monica 2001. p 49-50.

12. O'balance. Op. cit..p 53-54.

13. ibid. p 63.

14. Galula op. cit. p 52 - 53.

15. Joint Doctrine on Sub Conventional Warfare. HQ Integrated Defence Staff Delhi. p 39.

16. ibid. p 22.

17. Peterson, Reinhardt and Conger. Symposium on the Role of Air Power in Counterinsurgency and Unconventional Warfare: The Malayan Emergency. The Rand Corporation, Santa Monica California. p- 7. http://www.rand.org/pubs/research_memoranda/2005/RM3651.pdf. Accessed on 14 October 2011. Colonel RL Clutterbuck, O.B.E,Royal Engineers, served on the staff of the Director of Operations in Malaya as General Staff Officer, Grade 1, Plans, beginning 1956.

18. Op.cit. Pike Douglas. p 219

19. Mao Tse Tung Selected Military Writings of Mao Tse Tung, Bejing Foreign Language Press 1967. p 410.

20. Byman Daniel, Chalk Peter, Hoffman Bruce, Rosenaun William & Brannan David.op.cit. p 71.

21. Mao. Op. cit. p 155.

22. Ibid. p 159.

The Algerian Insurgency

Genesis of the Insurgency

The Algerian insurgency or war for independence began in 1954 and ended in 1962 after the French President Charles De Gaulle pronounced Algeria an independent country on 03July 1962. The history of French rule over Algeria goes back to June 1830, when the French landed at a Sidi Ferruch, a small coastal town in Algeria. Subsequently, on 04 March 1848, the French by a decree, declared Algeria as an 'integral part of France'[1]. Thus we see that Algeria was not a colony of France but a sovereign part of France. The French divided Algeria into three main regions (Oran, Algiers and Constantine, from west to east) as metropolitan departments.

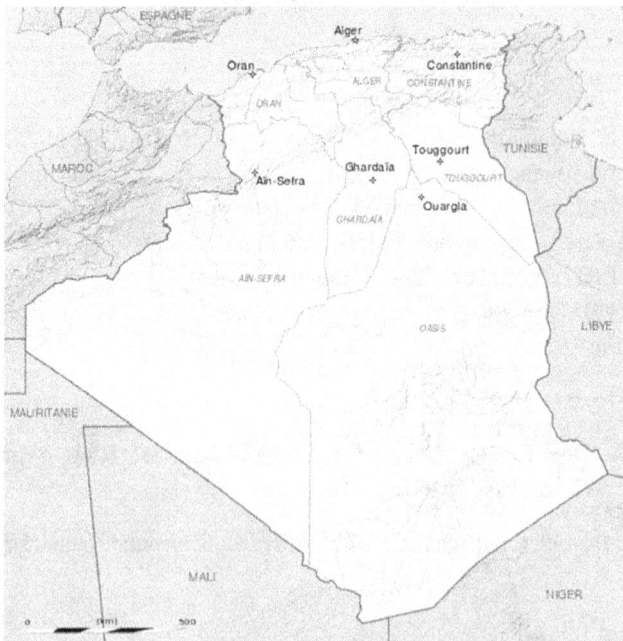

Map of Algeria[2]

The majority of population were native Moslems, mainly Arabs and Berbers[3], but they were dominated over by European settlers, known as "colons" or – more graphically – "pied noirs"[4]. Only a tiny minority of the Moslem population held French citizenship rights or significant property.

The population of Algeria was 86, 82,000, as per an official census taken in Algeria in October 1948. Of these, 77, 08,000 were Muslims and 9, 74,000 were Europeans. By 1954, the population had increased to 95,28,000 of which 84,86,000 were Moslem and only 10,42,000 were Europeans.[5] Despite Moslem majority, the Moslem suffered from chronic unemployment, poor health, and hunger and discrimination was prevalent. Politically, Algeria was an integral part of the French Republic rather than a colony. Its native Berber and Arab people were technically French citizens. But discrimination was rife The European immigrants, the *pied noires*, had a stranglehold on local government and police, farmed and owned most of the best arable land, enjoyed a virtual monopoly of political power and imposed their own educational, economic and administrative structures upon the domestic population .

Algerian nationalism before 1950s was split. Discontented Moslem had numerous parties from which to choose from –

- The Algerian Communist Party,

- The religious and pan-Islamic Association des Ulemas,

- The nationalistic Mouvementpur le Triomphe des Libertés Démocratiques (MTLD),

- The liberal Islamist Union Démocratique du Manifesto Algéria (UDMA)

None of these parties were offering policies with universal appeal. In 1949 the MTLD split when one of the leaders, Ben Bella[6] created the more militant Organisation Spéciale (OS), a party dedicated to the use of violence. The OS also did not attract widespread support. Although most of these parties attempted to participate in French political life, blatant electoral frauds by the colons prevented Muslim representation at all levels of government. The majority of pied noirs were nothing less volatile, headstrong, violent and unforgiving than the Moslem: they considered themselves as builders of Algeria and were fiercely determined to cling to what they had. Most of them considered any kind of compromise with Moslem as betrayal.

The MTLD was one of the first nationalist Algerian parties that became active. During WW-II, when the French were searching for volunteers amongst the Algerian population to help fight the Germans, many Algerian nationalists were given the promise that, if they would help in the war, Algeria would be given independence in return. After the war ended, the Algerians realised that the French were not serious in keeping their word. The MTLD organised demonstrations in Setif,[7]Batna Sedrata and Souk Ahras. The reaction of the French authorities and the pied noirs was fierce. In the ensuing reprisals several thousands of Moslems were killed.

Political divisions once again plagued the nationalist movements in the wake of the war. Mainstream parties encouraged moderate views, leaning towards peaceful negotiations for political association with the French. A small group broke ranks in 1946 and militated for independence through armed insurgency. Although this group's back was soon broken by the French police, its leaders escaped and found refuge in Egypt within the ranks of the Moslem Brotherhood. When France experienced a humiliating defeat in Indo china, withdrawing in the summer of 1954, Algerian radicals saw their opportunity and took it. They publicly announced the founding of the *Front de libération national* (FLN)[8].

The Armée De LibérationNationale (ALN)

The French estimated the size of the ALN in the beginning of the insurgency as 40,000. By the end of the insurgency, they estimated that only 10,000 to 12,000 insurgents were left.[9] Initially, the soldiers were armed with basic weapons such as hunting rifles and knives. Subsequently arms caches hidden during the Second World War also fell into the hands of the ALN. The ALN also raided French Army Depots for weapons. The ALN claimed that a lot of their arms were captured from attacks on the French.[10] In due course of time, the hunting guns were replaced by more sophisticated weapons such as the rifle, light and heavy machine guns, bazookas and mortars. By 1959, the ALN had also procured Piper Cub aircraft for liaison and observation roles. Arms may also have come from Communist China.[11] A lot of the weapons were also obtained from Czechoslovakia.[12] These weapons found their way into Algeria through Egypt after Gamal Abdel Nasser, the President of Egypt, made an arms agreement with Czechoslovakia.[13]

The ALN were inspired by the teachings of Mao Tse-tung and other texts on guerrilla warfare such as the Yugoslavian guerrilla war. The French Resistance also influenced their vocabulary and gave them words such as *maquis*.[14] The Algerian insurgency was modelled on Mao's teachings on insurgency.[15]

- The ***strategic defence*** required the insurgents to concentrate on gathering popular support and establishing its bases, low-level violence only for easy, lucrative targets, and mere survival.

- The ***strategic stalemate*** is characterized by mainly guerrilla warfare focusing on eroding the government's legitimacy and power while attempting to continue the mustering of forces in which the conventional army is recruited.

- The ***strategic offensive*** has the insurgents graduating from guerrilla warfare to conventional attacks to complete the collapse of the government.

The insurgency did not follow this model in the true spirit and often jumped stages before the conditions were correct. In 1959, the insurgents were forced to move back to the strategic defence from the strategic stalemate stage in order to survive. In the last stages the insurgency was on the defensive and finally defeated.[16]

The insurgents' tactics changed with time. They started off with small skirmishes and assassinations. With time, they escalated to operations with insurgents in uniform mounting Company sized operations with heavier armament. Towards the end of the insurgency, operations had reduced to small groups of 12 to 15 men. There were also incidents of terrorism in the cities.[17]

The Insurgency

In the early morning hours of 01 November 1954, the National Liberation Front (Front de LibérationNationale-FLN) launched around thirty attacks throughout Algeria in the opening salvo of the insurgency against military and police targets.[18]The reaction of not only the French authorities, but also the pied noirs, was fierce: in the ensuing revenge several thousands of Muslims were killed. Settlements inaccessible to the French Army including some 40 different villages were bombed by French Air Force SBD-5 Dauntless dive-bombers.

The FLN's strategy was to conduct a general uprising consisting of coordinated attacks throughout Algeria with announcements throughout the Arab world that the war for Algerian independence had begun.[19]In order to combat the French Army, the strategy was to start from a series of guerrilla bases, gain popular support, and harass and tie down French forces while building a conventional force that could eventually counter the French Army.The FLN also intended to use terrorism as a tactic and a strategy against French forces and the neutral population.

The insurgents harassed the French army, police, and administration through direct and indirect military action, sabotage, assassination, and terror. The ALN operating in the countryside needed support. Food for the ALN was not a problem as they were able to live off the land with the assistance of the civilian population. Recruitment was also not a problem as most of the Muslims were sympathetic to the FLN cause. The primary problem faced by the ALN was maintaining the supply of weapons and ammunition from abroad.[20]

French Counterinsurgency Response

In general, the French operations against the insurgency were initially limited. The French government did not initially accept or appreciate the real extent of the insurgency or take it seriously. It was evident that the insurgency was growing, but the French were hesitant in formally accepting the truth and declaring a state of emergency and permitting the security forces in conducting counterinsurgency operations as they are supposed to be conducted.[21] The French response was reactionary to any attack by the FLN.[22]

Subsequently, French strategy to defeat the insurgency in Algeria remained fairly consistent throughout the operations, although the tactics changed. The basic strategy was to end the insurgency by force, rendering the rebels incapable of maintaining a sustained and effective insurrection while simultaneously devising measures to win Muslim support. The French termed this strategy as 'Pacification'. They realised that the population was one of the main centres of gravity in the fight against insurgency.[23]

The French army had four main missions[24] –

- Defence of the Moroccan and Tunisian borders.
- Protection of the population of villages and towns.
- Provide a reserve for General Challe for counterinsurgency operations.
- Provide support units to the army, navy and air force.

The French used a new tactic they called as the Quadrillage (grid) tactic. *Quadrillage*[25] was a "grid operation", garrisoning all major cities, towns, villages, and farms of Algeria. *Quadrillage* tactics were supposed to isolate the insurgents by physically denying them popular support of the peasants towards the insurgency by providing civic actions. This tactic left fewer troops available for operations as it tied down many of them. However, it was reasonably successful.[26] French troops were able to capture and kill the insurgents in the countryside.

Another important part of the French pacification effort was isolation of the battlefield from external support. On Algeria's eastern border with Tunisia, the French constructed a long series of heavily fortified positions known as the Morice Line, in order to stop the flow of men material and other resources from Tunisia. Facing a similar problem of external support from Morocco on the western border, the French built the Pedron Line.

The Morice Line consisted of two electric fences ten metres apart with barbed wire entanglements some thirty metres in front. The French placed approximately three million land mines between the barbed wire and the fences to complete the physical obstruction. Each day, the border force ploughed a ten-metre strip inside the barricade to allow trackers to assess the size of any groups that successfully crossed the line. In places, the security forces cleared the civilian population to a depth of thirty to fifty miles, thereby denying intelligence to the insurgents. Sensors and alarms alerted mechanised reaction forces, whilst prepared tracks allowed for a rapid response to incursions. Tanks, armoured cars, infantry units and aircraft patrolled the border areas, firing at anything that moved.This made it nearly impossible for the insurgents to obtain external support from across the borders.

Having sealed the borders, the French Army moved to pacify the rest of the country and provide protection to the populace from the FLN. The French devised a program called the Regroupment Programme. In this, large portions of the local population were forcibly concentrated in camps under military supervision to prevent them from voluntarily aiding the rebels. In the three years (1957–60) during which the *regroupement* program was followed, more than one million Algerians were removed from their villages.[27]

By 1960, the French had won the insurgency on the ground but lost the battle politically. The military forces of the FLN were defeated and demoralised. However, on the political front, the FLN was still very much active. The United Nations (UN) and other countries sided with the FLN and voiced opposition to French rule in Algeria.With the pressure from the UN, Charles de Gaulle realised that maintaining French rule in Algeria was a lost cause. On 18 March, 1962, the French declared a cease fire.

The Use of Air Power by the French Air Force

The Algerian conflict offers a very valuable insight, relevant to the conduct of counterinsurgency operations in today's security environment. The French Air Force (FAF) maintained a peace time role in Algeria before the insurgency. The air force resources were limited. The peace time tasks assigned to the air force were-

- Air defence.
- Transport support.

- Any other mission to ensure French sovereignty.

Organisation of French Air Force

After the insurgency broke out in Algeria, the French Air Force in Algeria was reorganised to provide effective support and be more flexible and responsive, two very important characteristics of air power. A requirement was felt to structure the FAF so as to be able to provide the ground forces with sufficient air support. Heading military operations was a Commander – in – Chief with a Joint Staff who had authority over the army, navy and air force. They were responsible for preparing and maintaining the forces of the Tenth Military Region of the Army and the Fifth Air Region of the Air Force. However, they were not responsible for the conduct of operations. At the operational level, there were three Tactical Air Commands and Army Corps for the three regions of Oran, Algeria and Constantine. Each Tactical Air Command and Army Corps had its own Joint Operations Centre from where very close co-operation was maintained. These two Commands generally were located in the same building. At the next lower level, there was an Advance Air Command located at Divisional level with the Joint Operations Centre also located in the same building. At the ground level, the Commander of a particular operation was assisted by an Air Directing Post. A very important aspect of this decentralised structure was that all the Tactical Air Commands were provided with the resources. The Fifth Air Region only maintained the resources for the conduct of Air Defence missions. In addition, a system was devised amongst the Tactical Air Commands for providing reciprocal aid whenever a situation arose. This could be achieved from 15 to 20 minutes to a few hours depending on the distance. Most of the aircraft available in Algeria were dispersed. This was done so as to give the Advance Air Commands at the Divisional level the flexibility of using air power as per the situation. The deployment was altered as per the situation on ground. Thus we see that the organisation was tailored to ensure a very high level of flexibility.

Command and Control

The command of the air assets was with the Tactical Air Commander. Initially, the army aircraft were under army command. Subsequently they came under the Tactical Air Commander. To ensure a very reactive command and control organisation, the FAF had a highly developed network of radio communication. An extensive network of VHF communication existed to facilitate air to ground communication. The French located VHF antennae on high ground to ensure effective VHF communication and radio relay throughout the insurgency effected areas. They had extensive RT coverage at 1,000 feet, covering areas up to 250 Km by 280 Km.[28] Aircraft and ground RT sets were common.

The air support network was open 24 hours. A request for air support was thus received simultaneously at the Army Division, Air Command Post and the Tactical Air Command. As a result of this, air support would normally be sent by the Tactical Air Command at the Corps level even before the Advance Air Command at the Divisional level could react. The Tactical Air Commander had a situation map at the Joint Operations Centre to identify all aircraft. As General YP Ezanno, the Commander of the Second Tactical Air Group in Algeria from 1957 to 1959 said:

> "*I often would send aircrafts even before the Division reaction. Our antennas were located on high terrain and from my Headquarters we could monitor everything.*"[29]

This was also communicated to the Joint Operations Centre at the Division. As a result of this agile control set up, a Company under attack from the insurgents was also able to call for air support, without having to process the request upwards. At times, air support was immediately available from airborne aircraft.

FAF Resources

In the beginning of 1959, the FAF had 801 aircraft consisting of fighters, transport, light observation planes and helicopters. In addition, the Army Aviation maintained around 100 helicopters and 120 light observation liaison aircraft. The Navy had 36 helicopters and ten aircraft for maritime surveillance.[30]

FAF Roles

The FAF in Algeria was organised to be flexible to the requirements of the ground forces, especially at the lower levels. The roles of the FAF during the insurgency were–

- Intelligence collection and Reconnaissance
- Air borne Assault
- Air Transport operations
- Close Air Support (CAS)
- Interdiction

Reconnaissance

One of the most important roles was aerial reconnaissance with the aim of detecting the insurgents and gathering intelligence on them. In 1959 itself, a total of 34,500 reconnaissance missions totalling 73,000 hours were carried out.[31] This reconnaissance was usually carried out by light observation aircraft. The French carried out photographic mapping of large areas which were suspected of being insurgent infested. They also used to carry out regular visual reconnaissance missions aiming to establish the behavioural pattern of the population. Each pilot was assigned a specific area which he observed daily, flying at irregular intervals. Visual reports were at times by taking photographs from the air using hand held cameras. This helped the French to determine the routine activities of the locals and immediately be able to discern any suspicious movement. By these efforts, the French were able to obtain very valuable information, at times even being able to identify the building in which the insurgents were holding a meeting. By building up on the behaviour pattern of the locals and its analysis, intelligence inputs were obtained much faster.

To spot insurgents movements along the borders and control infiltration before the Morice line was constructed, jets were used to carry out border patrols and reconnaissance. The flat terrain lent itself to this type of reconnaissance. The jets could not be heard till it was too late for the people to hide. These jets were also fitted with external tanks to increase theirrange and endurance. After the Morice line was built, night aerial reconnaissance was carried out using flares.

Airborne Assault

Airborne assault missions were undertaken to quickly move in troops to an area where aerial surveillance had picked up the presence of insurgents. One of the important lessons learnt by the French was that any movement of ground forces by surface transport was instantaneously detected by the insurgents. The insurgents would immediately come to know of the operation. Therefore, all transport movement was stopped by the army before launching any operation.

Airborne assault missions were planned after referring to aerial photographs. Having identified the area for the airborne troops to be dropped, the area surrounding it would be interdicted by fighter bombers or aircraft like the T-6 in order to sanitise it. Insurgents fleeing the area were also interdicted from the air. The aim of this exercise was to induct the ground forces into the operational area only after clearing the drop zones of insurgents.

To avoid ground fire, the helicopters flying in the troops would transit at 1500 feet. Routes were planned as far as possible to avoid over flying areas with known insurgent presence.[32] The heli-borne troops would arrive in a timed interval of two minutes just after the initial bombing. The timing of two minutes was found to be important as the insurgents would otherwise recover and send in suicidal troops to shoot down the helicopters while they were disembarking the heli-borne troops. The helicopter in the lead would have control over the mission. Every fifth helicopter would be armed. Armed helicopters provided close air support to the landing soldiers, sanitising the area around it. The helicopter guns which were removable and mounted on the side were found to be more effective than the axially mounted ones. The helicopter, while firing at a target would orbit around it with the side gun always firing at the target. To protect the aircrew, thick nylon lining the seats capable of stopping bullets up to 8 mm, was used.[33] The French pilots also wore bullet proof jackets for self-protection. Such operations were found to be very successful by the French. In one such operation, the French were able to kill 197 insurgents, and capture 60 of them against a loss of only two killed and ten injured.[34]By employing armed helicopters to sanitise the landing area, the FAF practically suffered no loss of helicopters.

Close Air Support

Another important role carried out by the FAF was close air support (CAS). As brought out earlier, a very effective communication system existed between the ground troops and the FAF. This enabled the troops on the ground to demand for immediate air support enabling them to receive fire support from the air and neutralise the insurgents. Where ever insurgents were concentrated in caves in cliffs and mountains, armed helicopters used the SS – 10[35] or SS – 11[36] missiles to destroy their positions.[37] Command and control of the situation switched between the lead helicopter and the ground forces and vice versa as per requirement. The system was fluid, efficient, and effective. This capability gave French forces a tremendous advantage. Napalm bombs and bombs with a delay fuse were also used against the insurgents. Bomber aircraft like the A-26 were pressed into action against villages when the French troops came under attack. Such attacks had an adverse effect and they destroyed schools and many civilian casualties occurred. It brought negative publicity to the French and also strengthened the support of the local population towards the insurgents. They also used these bombers to interdict the ALN arms supply lines from across the Morice Line by as much as 70 %.[38]

Air Transport

A subordinate Air Transport Command to the one that was based in Paris operated under the control of the Fifth Air Region in Algeria. It had three squadrons, of which two were based in Algiers and one in Blida (a city located about 45 km south-west of Algiers). Each squadron had 16 Noratlas aircrafts.[39]

Air transport missions also operated between Paris and Algeria. They did not face any major problems. There was no threat of enemy air action over Algeria, weather was favourable to air operations most of the year, except for four months of bad weather and co-ordination with civil air traffic was not a constraint due to the light intensity of civil traffic. The only difficulty faced in air transport operations was keeping the air crew at a high level of training. Only five hours a month were dedicated to training. Another problem faced by aircrew was the psychological factor of having to adjust between peace time missions from Paris to Algeria and thereafter being inducted into operations.[40]

Air transport missions comprised most importantly of movement of troops and para dropping supplies by day and at times by night and CasEvac of troops. Both fixed wing and helicopters were utilised in these roles. The insertion of troops directly into battle was found to be very beneficial as it ensured a high degree of surprise and concentration of forces and ensuring that the troops arrived fresh and not fatigued after long marches. Mobile beacons (Rebecca system[41]) were used to navigate to the drop zones for resupplying troops.

Concluding Observations

The operations in Algeria have brought out the importance of joint ground and air operations in fighting the insurgency. The majority of air operations such as air transport, close air support and reconnaissance were joint in nature. Colonel Rene Laure described counter guerrilla warfare as," *a combined Air-Army problem requiring a lot of imagination and co-operation – a human problem rather than a technical problem.*"[42]

The importance of good air to ground communication has been adequately emphasised. By siting antennae on high ground, the French were able to ensure that a request for air support was received simultaneously at the Army Division, Air Command Post and the Tactical Air Command. This reduced the reaction time for providing air support to the troops. Any reconnaissance pilot could also radio in for air support from a height of 1000 feet or more. This ensured that the pilot never lost sight of the insurgent movement.

Aerial reconnaissance missions were very useful as most counter-insurgency operations were based on information collected from these missions. Air patrols could cover large areas which were not patrolled by ground forces. The pilots became familiar with the pattern of life followed by the population. Any irregular activity usually provided an indication for insurgent activity.

Patrolling of the fences helped in keeping its integrity and avoided it being breeched by insurgents and foreign supporters, trying to smuggle in arms and ammunition into Algeria.

Armed helicopters were used extensively in conjunction with ground forces in encircling the insurgents and tightening the noose around them. Fighter bomber aircraft sanitised the landing just prior to the troop carrying helicopters. An armed helicopter would subsequently disembark the troops helping in combing operations. These helicopters were subsequently always available for close air support to the ground forces.

Endnotes

1   Gillespie Joan: Algeria Rebellion and Revolution, Earnest Benn Limited, 1960,p 7

2   http://en.wikipedia.org/wiki/File:French_Algeria_1934-1955_administrative_map-fr.svg. Assessed on 09 January 2013.

3   Berbers are the indigenous people of North Africa west of the Nile Valley.

4   Pied-Noir ("Black-Foot"), plural Pieds-Noirs, pronounced [pjenwa☐], is a term referring to French citizens of various origins who lived in French Algeria before independence. Specifically, Pieds-Noirs include those of European settlers descent from France or other European countries (such as Spain, Italy and Malta), who were born in Algeria.

5   Gillespie, op. cit. , p 29.

6   Mohamed Ahmed Ben Bella (Muhammad Ahmad Bin Balla) born on 25 December 1918, Maghnia, Algeria was a soldier and Algerian revolutionary, who became the first President of Algeria.

7   On 8 May 1945, the day of the formal end of World War II in Europe, an uprising against the occupying French forces in Sétif and the nearby towns Guelma and Kherrata resulted in the deaths of 104 pieds-noirs. The uprising was suppressed through what is now known as the Sétif massacre.

8   The National Liberation Front French: Front de Libération Nationale, hence FLN) is a socialist political party in Algeria. It was set up as a merger of other smaller groups, to obtain independence for Algeria from France. The FLN's armed wing during the war was called the Armée de Libérationnationale(ALN).

9   Peterson AH, Reinhardt GC and Conger EE, Symposium on the Role of Airpower in Counterinsurgency and Unconventional Warfare: The Algerian

War, The Rand Corporation 1963, p 6-8.

10   O'Ballance Edgar: The Algerian Insurrection1954-1962,Faber and Faber 24 Russell Square London 1967, p 121.

11   Gillespie, op. cit. , p 107-111.

12   Peterson AH, Reinhardt GC and Conger EE, op. cit. p 10.

13   O'Ballance Edgar: op. cit., p50-51.

14   The Maquis (French pronunciation: [ma□ki]) were the predominantly rural guerrilla bands of the French Resistance. Initially they were composed of men who had escaped into the mountains to avoid conscription to provide forced labour for Germany during WW - II.

15   O'Ballance op. cit., p 50-51.

16   Ibid.,p11

17   Peterson AH, Reinhardt GC and Conger EE, op. cit. p 11.

18   Gillespie, op. cit. , p 95.

19   O'Ballance op. cit., p 50.

20   Peterson AH, Reinhardt GC and Conger EE, op. cit. p 10

21   O'Balance, op. cit. , p 50 – 52.

22   Galula David: Pacification in Algeria 1954-1958, Rand Corporation, p 51.

23   Ibid. p xx.

24   Peterson AH, Reinhardt GC and Conger EE, op. cit. p 13.

25   General Raoul Salan, commanding the French Army in Algeria, instituted a system of Quadrillage, dividing the country into sectors, each permanently garrisoned by troops responsible for suppressing insurgent operations in their assigned territory.

26   O'Balance, op. cit. , p 78

27   Ibid. p 137.

28   Peterson AH, Reinhardt GC and Conger EE, op. cit. p 27

29   ibid. p 23.

30   ibid. p 21.

31   TiwaryArun Kumar Air Commodore: Air Power and Counter Insurgency,

Lancer Books PO Box 4236, New Delhi, p78.

32   Peterson AH, Reinhardt GC and Conger EE, op. cit. p 37.

33   Tiwary.Op. Cit. p 79.

34   Peterson AH, Reinhardt GC and Conger EE, op. cit. p 37.

35   The SS – 10 is a French wire guided anti-tank missile. The FAF modified their helicopters to carry up to four of these missiles. SS stands for Sol-Sol" French for Surface to Surface.

36   The SS - 11 was intended as a heavy version of the SS.10 for use from vehicles, ships and helicopters, with even an infantry version developed later. The missile entered service with the French army under the designation SS.11. It was used as the first helicopter-mounted anti-tank missile in the world.

37   Peterson AH, Reinhardt GC and Conger EE, op. cit..p 41.

38   Mark R Heusinkveld, Major: The Role Of Light Attack/Armed Reconnaissance Aircraft In Counterinsurgency: A Comparative Case Study Of Algeria And The Vietnam War, Fort Leavenworth, Kansas 2010-02. p 19.

39   Peterson AH, Reinhardt GC and Conger EE, op. cit. p 45.The Nord Noratlas was a 1950s French military transport aircraft. It had two Hercules 4,000 horsepower engines, could carry 32 seated passengers or 20-32 armed paratroopers with their individual equipment. The aircraft could operate from most of the airfields in Algeria.

40   Ibid. p-47.

41   The Rebecca/Eureka system was a transponder system used as a radio homing beacon by means of a Eureka ground emitter responding to queries from an airborne Rebecca interrogator.

42   Peterson AH, Reinhardt GC and Conger EE, op. cit. p- 72. Colonel Rene Laure of the French Army commanded a brigade in Algeria.

The Malayan Emergency

The Malayan Emergency was declared on 17 June 1948[1] by the British High Commissioner, after three estate managers were murdered in Perak, northern Malaya. The men were murdered by guerrillas of the Malayan Communist Party (MCP). On 23 July 1948, the MCP was declared to be an unlawful society.[2]

The history of British colonisation in Malaya dates back to 1786, when Penang was ceded to Britain. In the ensuing years, the British entered into treaties with the various state rulers in Malaya, taking the mantle of a protecting power.

Map of Malaya[3]

Malaya had rich Tin ore deposits and rubber plantations which helped the British to flourish in Malaya. The Malayan people had an easygoing nature, content with their small farms and fishing businesses. Cheap labour was available from China and India, which went back to their respective countries after earning money. Many Chinese also stayed back, did well and transformed themselves into a flourishing commercial society.

The MCP was formed in 1930 with an aim of trying to control the Chinese population in Malaya. A young Vietnamese called Lai Tek was elected the Secretary General of the MCP in 1939. In 1941, after the Japanese invaded Malaya, the MCP offered help to the British in fighting the Japanese, including organising guerrilla warfare behind the Japanese army lines. The British, on their part, agreed to train and arm the MCP guerrillas. This led to the creation of the Malayan People's Anti-Japanese Army (MPAJA), which had a strength of about 7,000 men.[4] This organisation had a dual aim of evicting the Japanese from Malaya and subsequently the British. The Japanese surrendered in August 1945 to the Allies. The MCP agreed to co-operate in re-establishing British rule and they disbanded the guerrilla army, albeit reluctantly. The MCP returned a lot of arms which had been supplied by the British but at the same time, retained a large stockpile of arms and ammunition in the jungle, which had been left behind by the Japanese. The MCP could therefore equip its guerrilla regiments when necessary.

Post World War II, the Chinese community in Malaya had many grievances, the chief one being that they were not allowed to hold government posts and the denial of full citizenship. The MCP was able to convince the Chinese population that they would be second class citizens until the MCP came into power. The MCP resorted to organising strikes and subverting trade unions. However the government was able to keep these activities under control.

The final objective of the MCP was to overthrow the Government of Malaya and establish a Communist Republic of Malaya. This objective was never lost sight of. It is believed that the decision to take up an armed insurgency was taken at the Communist Youth Conference held at Calcutta.[5] This conference was held from 19

February 1948 to 24 February 1948 and was sponsored by the World Federation of Democratic Youth (WFDY) and the Conference of Youth and Students of South-East Asia fighting for Freedom and Independence.[6] Lai Tek, the Secretary General of the MCP had been replaced by Chin Peng in 1947. He initially tried to over throw the government by organising strikes and subversive activities, as brought out, which did not succeed. By 1948, the MCP shifted its strategy of armed violence and riots by unarmed crowds.[7]

The guerrilla fighters of the MPAJA were remobilised. A new organisation called the Malayan Peoples Anti-British Army (MPABA) was formed. Overthrowing British rule was to be carried out as per the teachings of Mao Tse-tung.

- **Phase 1.** The battle hardened, ex MPAJA guerrilla fighters, would raid isolated estates, tin mines and police and government buildings in rural areas to drive the British into the cities

- **Phase 2.** The areas abandoned by the British would be renamed 'Liberated areas' and guerrilla bases would be established for military expansion and training of new recruits

- **Phase 3.** The final phase was to defeat the British Malaya Army.

Counterinsurgency Operations

A state of Emergency was declared on 23 July 1948. The civil government was in control throughout with the army assisting them. This gave legal backing to the police and military action in defeating the insurgency and controlling the violence. Numerous measures were adopted. The important ones were:-

Registration of Population. The entire population above the age of twelve was required to register themselves at the nearest police station. They were photographed and their thumb impressions taken and subsequently issued with identity cards which they were required to carry at all times. The people who did not register themselves were put under surveillance. Registration of the population hampered the activities and movement of the communists, despite all their efforts to sabotage the process. Guerrillas found it difficult to move freely and anyone found outside his normal neighbourhood was put under suspicion, thereby building up intelligence. Without Registration Cards, the locals could not buy food and rations nor participate in a host of other activities. This was the incentive to the villagers to register themselves and safeguard their cards. Registration of the population was effective in ensuring that the communist found it difficult to live in the villages with the people and obtain food and intelligence.

Power to Arrest. The next important step taken was giving the police the power to arrest suspects and detain them without a trial. This assisted the police in detaining communists against whom they had enough circumstantial evidence, but would not stand in a court of law to obtain a conviction.

Power to Search Private Property. The police were given powers to search private property without a warrant. This helped the police in carrying out random snap checks and it led to the arrest of communist guerrillas.

The Briggs Plan

By 1950, the British were fighting a losing battle. Though they were killing guerrillas, the communists were also making up for their losses by recruitment. There was a danger of the government losing the faith of the people, giving victory to the communists. The communist guerrillas were getting sufficient food, clothing and intelligence from the people, despite all the efforts of the police in controlling the situation. In April 1950, General Sir Harold Briggs was appointed as Director of Operations and to act as the executive of the High Commissioner. He was given control over the police, army and air force and the authority to co-ordinate operations with the civil government in the counterinsurgency operations. The main aspects of the Briggs Plan as it came to be called were:[8]

- Domination of the populated areas to provide security to the people so as to enable the steady and increasing flow of intelligence and information coming from all sources.

- Fragmentation of the Communist organisations within the populated areas.

- Preventing the supply of food and other requirements to the Communist Guerrillas from populated areas.

- Neutralising the guerrillas by forcing them to attack the security forces on their own ground.

The overall aim of the Briggs Plan was to weaken the Communist Guerrillas, by a combination of direct ground and air operations, and indirectly, by denying them their sources of supply and support. The Brigg's Plan was ultimately successful.

The Role of Air Power

Before bringing out the role of airpower in combating the insurgency, a word on the predicaments experienced by the ground forces needs to be mentioned. The Malayan jungles are thick and difficult to penetrate. The insurgents knew the jungle better than the security forces. The security forces had to learn how to defeat the communist insurgents (also called the Communist Terrorists (CTs) by the British) in the jungle. Advancing in the jungle was a gruelling task, especially with no roads and few tracks. Hence, vehicular movement was more or less non-existent. Supplies were limited; therefore, the ground forces needed some way to be resupplied, in order to move forward.

Air Commodore PE Warcup, CBE, who commanded the RAF in Kuala Lumpur between 1957 and 1959, said, on the role of airpower during the Emergency in Malaya, "*The Air Force gave them (ground forces) the necessities of life and enabled them to carry out their task in the jungle. If then the ground forces were the killing instrument, the role of the RAF was one of complete- and I say complete - support to them. The main killing weapons were the ground forces, supported by the air, with both always acting in concert with the political objective.*"[9]Thus we see that the main role of the Air Force was in support of the ground forces.

Air power was effectively utilised for air supply of garrisons, patrols, rapid movement of troops, reconnaissance, psychological warfare and offensive air strikes. One of the most effective roles was also being able to project government control and providing government services to remote areas, deep in the jungle.[10] This helped in winning over the aborigines who were being utilised by the communist forces.

Organisation and Forces

The RAF was commanded by an Air Commodore, who was stationed at Kuala Lumpur. The Air Officer Commanding (AOC) the RAF was also a member of the Director of Operations Committee. The Senior Air Staff Officer, who was responsible for the operational aspects, had a Joint Operations Centre (JOC), which was staffed with Army and Air Force officers. The JOC was headed by a Wing Commander.

The JOC was manned by a Squadron Leader, a Major G-3 Operations and a Flight Lieutenant, Intelligence. The Flight Lieutenant maintained a situation board on which the air operations effort was kept updated and a daily air intelligence summary prepared. All requests for offensive air missions or transport missions were received at the JOC, where they would be prioritised, allotted resources and issued with orders.

The forces under the command of the AOC comprised of units from the Royal Air Force, Royal Australian Air Force and Royal New Zealand Air Force. All the aircraft were stationed at Kuala Lumpur. The aircraft deployed in Malaya were:[11]

- Avro Lincoln the attack role.[12]

- Bristol Brigands (equivalent to an American B-26).[13]

- Bristol Beaufighter.[14]

- de'Havilland Hornets.[15]

- de'Havilland Mosquito.[16]

- de'Havilland Vampires.[17]

- Hawker Tempests.[18]

- Gloster Meteor.[19]

- Vickers Valetta.[20]

- Sunderland flying boats[21]

- Dakota transport aircraft.[22]

- Scottish Aviation Pioneer aircraft.[23]

- Auster aircraft.[24]

- Westland Dragonfly helicopters.[25]

- Westland Whirlwind helicopters.[26]

- Towards the end of the insurgency, Sabre (F-86)[27] squadrons and Canberra[28] squadrons were also deployed.

Impediments to Air Operations

There were two major impediments while conducting air operations in Malaya. The first one was the weather. There were no accurate or reliable meteorological forecasts. Pilots were required to get airborne, assess the weather and then carry out their missions. Adverse weather such as cumulus or low clouds would build up very quickly; affecting the safe conduct of the mission. The second problem area was navigation. There were no navigational aids such as homers or beacons at the beginning of the insurgency. Pilots were required to navigate by dead reckoning and by reading maps, a very difficult task over thick jungle which hardly had any land marks. As such, the maps were not very accurate. The third problem faced by the pilots was fatigue. In the hot and humid climate of Malaya, the pilots lost an average of three pounds of weight in a two and a half hour sortie.

Transport Operations

Air supply operations for the ground forces operating in the thick jungles formed the most important part of air transport operations during the Malayan Emergency. The ground forces operating in small size patrols could at the utmost carry supplies for seven days.[29] By resupplying them from the air, time was not a constraint for the patrols and they could operate independently till they completed the mission.

Supplies were usually packed in packs weighing up to 200 pounds, which could be dropped from the aircraft by parachute. Dropping zones were usually just 100 square yards in dimension and the drops were carried out from 200 feet above the trees. The drops were fairly accurate, indicating the skills of the pilot and dispatcher. The Dakota aircraft which was also utilised for this role was well suited for it with its low speed handling capability and small radius of turn. It did have a few disadvantages such as a low rate of climb, which was required while exiting from valley drops and reduced forward and downward visibility, which hampered the accuracy of air drops.

Requests for air supplies were made by the ground forces to their respective police or army headquarters through their respective communication nets. The supplies would be prepared and loaded onto the aircraft by the Royal Army Supply Corps. The JOC would be informed about the location for the drop. The supply aircraft and the ground forces were able to communicate with each other over radio. These radios sets were old and gave a lot of problems. The ground forces would fire a flare to help the pilots locate the drop zone. Most supply sorties made multiple drops, supplying different patrols. The supply drops did give away the position of the ground forces to the communist guerrillas. However, these patrols were never attacked while recovering the supplies. They would keep away from the patrols as the patrols would be on guard, waiting for any such attack. This procedure worked well. The progress of the ground forces depended on being resupplied from the air.[30] The scope of these operations grew from just 60,000 pounds delivered over the first six months of the conflict to over 700,000 pounds during a single month in 1954.[31] This brings out the importance of such operations.

The Pioneer aircraft, which was a Short Take Off and Landing (STOL) aircraft, was also used to resupply small garrison outposts deep in the jungle, which were also called 'jungle forts'. Small landing strips would be prepared of about 200 yards in length. This aircraft had the capacity to accommodate up to five passengers. It was found to be very useful in resupplying, and changing the garrison safely, without exposing the men to the CTs or an enforced march out of the jungle. The Pioneer aircraft was also utilised to familiarise personnel from the civil administration, police and even the army about the territory that they were going to operate in. The low speed characteristic of this aircraft was also exploited in locating insurgent camps deep in the jungle and marking them for being bombed. This was found to be difficult, even when flying at 80 knots speed.

The Valetta aircraft also played a sterling role in air transport operations. These aircrafts were able to air drop 4,000 tonnes of supplies and airlift 30,000 personnel with 250 tonnes of equipment.[32]

The Valetta was also used in the psychological warfare role. They dropped up to a million leaflets a day asking the insurgents to surrender and the advantages of doing so. This was found to be very effective in inducing the insurgents to surrender. The Valetta was initially modified to carry external loudspeakers to broadcast a taped message to the insurgents, urging them to surrender with the promise of general amnesty. Subsequently, the Dakota aircraft was used in this role as it was more effective. Army Auster aircrafts were also modified for this role by installing loudspeakers under their wings on the left side of the fuselage, The Auster which was popularly called the 'Voice Aircraft', could broadcast messages over areas where the Dakotas could not operate such as over jungle roads and edges. About 4,500 sorties in 4,000 hours of flying time was the effort dedicated towards psychological warfare.[33]Psychological warfare operations were very effective and the British realised the importance of these operations. By 1952 the morale of the insurgents severely dipped and the effectiveness of this method became obvious. In 1955, interrogation of captured insurgents revealed that 100 % of surrendered enemy personnel stated that they had heard propaganda being broadcasted from voice aircraft, many of whom agreed that these messages greatly influenced them in making a decision to surrender. The medium of the air was the only way in which psychological warfare could be employed in isolated populated areas and deep in the jungle.

Army Auster aircraft were utilised in the reconnaissance role. These aircrafts were located along with the army brigades and were under the control of the Brigade Commander. These were mainly utilised for carrying out reconnaissance of an area of about 150 miles by 60 miles. The aim of these sorties was to observe the pattern of life of designated areas. Every observation was meticulously recorded and plotted on a master map after the sortie and, changes studied. This gave a fairly good ground picture to the local commander. These air reconnaissance sorties were also very helpful in assisting ground patrols in navigating in the jungle by giving them their ground position and a compass bearing to their destination. Most available maps of Malaya were obsolete and of poor quality. Parts of the country had never been accurately surveyed and mapped. Photographic reconnaissance supported the revision of old maps and the preparation of new ones. Photo reconnaissance missions also assisted in building up intelligence regarding the pattern of life by revealing new trails and jungle cultivation but did not reveal too much intelligence on the movement of the insurgents.[34] They were very helpful in locating communist guerrilla camps. In a six month period in 1955, such sorties were able to locate 155 confirmed guerrilla camps and 77 probable camps.[35]

Pilots suffered a very high casualty rate of four times that of the infantry due to bad weather and hilly terrain.[36]Before going into operations, pilots underwent a small survival course at the Survival School. Thereafter, to familiarise them with the terrain, ground situation and stress upon them and the importance of accurate supply drops, newly arrived pilots were taken on a ground patrol for five to six days. This experience helped instil confidence in the pilots that they could survive in the jungle if the need arose. All aircrew flew with seat type survival packs attached to the parachute, while the other crew members had chest type survival packs. These survival packs were always strapped on during the mission.

Helicopter Operations

Malaya saw one of the first operational deployments of helicopters in the counterinsurgency role.[37] They were deployed in Malaya in 1953 and were instrumental in assisting the British defeat the communist insurgents.[38] In the words of Air Commodore PE Warcup, "*If the supply drops (from the air) gave the ground forces their sustenance, I suggest that the helicopters provided their mobility.*"[39]Apart from tactical troop mobility, helicopters were also used extensively in the Casualty Evacuation role.

The versatility of the helicopter in being able to operate in any kind of terrain was instrumental in bringing the war against insurgency to the doorstep of the insurgent in the jungle. Its ability of vertical landing, take-off and hover were ideally suited to the jungle terrain. If required, the ground forces would create landing areas by blowing up trees. This enhanced the mobility, flexibility, range and endurance of the ground forces. Before the helicopters were inducted into operations, troops were required to march through thick jungles to reach an area suspected to be insurgent infested. On reaching, invariably, the insurgents would have fled having been forewarned by the aborigines or having heard the ground patrols moving in the jungle. The most effective use of the helicopter was inserting the troops directly into the area of interest, without the enforced march through thick jungles, thereby ensuring their arrival, fresh, fully rationed, alert for battle and most importantly with complete surprise. The British were able to deploy a full battalion in the jungle by helicopters within a few hours.[40]

Igor Sikorsky, the Russian American pioneer in helicopter and fixed wing aviation, in 1947 had quoted, "If you are in trouble anywhere in the world, an aircraft can come and drop flowers, but a helicopter can land and save your life."[41] The helicopter is ideally suited in the Casualty Evacuation (Casevac) and Combat Search and Rescue (CSAR) roles. Helicopter operations were able to evacuate 4,579 casualties during the Malayan Emergency.[42]

With experience, new tactics were evolved in the use of helicopters in the offensive role. They were used very successfully in Command and Control ,and Cordon and Search operations. Controlled by the Commander, airborne and enjoying a bird's eye view, the troops would be initially deployed around the insurgents' positions by helicopters and subsequently redeployed. He would give his troops instructions by radio transmissions and redeploy them as and when required, in an effort to tighten the noose around the insurgents. Small clearings or openings in the jungle would be used, into which the troops would slither down ropes if the helicopter could not land. In the words of Brigadier RCH Miers, DSO and Bar, OBE, who commanded a battalion in Malaya, "*For my part it was, by any account, a unique experience in commanding ones battalion. No commander can hope to get a better view of his men going into action.*"[43]

In one operation against the insurgents, the success of the operation was primarily due to the use of airpower in the three roles of reconnaissance, bombing and troop deployment. A reconnaissance aircraft picked up the signs of an insurgent camp which was correlated with other intelligence inputs and confirmed. The camp and its surrounding area was bombed from the air and thereafter troops were deployed using helicopters for cordon and search operations so as to capture the surviving insurgents.[44]

Another helicopter role was crop spraying. The insurgents had started cultivating crops in jungle clearings for food. In an attempt to curtail the ability of the insurgents to survive in the jungle, food denial became a crucial operation against the guerrillas. Helicopters sprayed toxic chemicals on these cultivation sites. These missions started in 1952, and by the end of the next year 88 sites had been destroyed.[45]

Helicopters were located centrally at Singapore. Subsequently, they were deployed at Kuala Lumpur under the control of the JOC. By not deploying them in forward positions, many flying hours were lost in moving them to the area of interest. This limitation was imposed due to the paucity of this resource. With an increase in the strength of helicopters, some were deployed up front. However, they were serviced centrally. Refuelling at forward locations was not found to be a problem as the police would assist by positioning the fuel at designated areas.

Another role in which the helicopter was utilised was in winning the hearts and minds of the people.[46] They were used in flying wounded civilians to hospitals or flying in medical supplies and doctors. This would have gone a long way in denying the insurgents in gaining the support of the people in remote areas.

Offensive Air Support

The aim of offensive air operations was to destroy the insurgent camps and equipment and kill as many of them as possible, or, to flush them out by strafing them into an area desired by the police or army. At times, bombing or dropping flares was resorted to increasing the nuisance value for the insurgents by keeping them awake throughout the night and thus reducing their morale. For the success of these operations, a pre-requisite was accurate intelligence regarding their exact location, and thereafter the ability to navigate accurately to these camps and identify them from the air. The British were also constrained in bombing to ensure that the pro-government population were not injured or the rubber plantations or factories damaged. All offensive air missions were required to be cleared by the police and a District Committee which included a District Officer. This District Officer was a kind of a friend and guide to the local population. This was to ensure that friendly areas were not bombed and damaged.

The British employed two methods for bombing. The first, which was not very accurate required the target to be marked by a reconnaissance aircraft, with smoke or flares. The second was by controlling the strike aircraft by radar to a pre-determined point at which the bombs were released. The efficacy of these area bombing operations in neutralising the insurgents was questionable. One of the squadrons operating with eight aircrafts, over an eight year period, dropped 17,500 tonnes of bombs and was able to confirm that 16 insurgents had been killed.[47] Despite the inaccuracies, the bombing did have positive results. As per a Major in the British Army, "*I hope that it is explained to the pilots that, far from being a waste of time, this area strafing is of vital importance in South Selangor where the troops are so thin on the ground that virtually the only hope of ground contact with the gang lies in the successful denial to them of as many jungle portions of the area as possible. If they are disappointed that they cannot have pinpoint targets and the satisfaction of killing bandits, they must be consoled with the thought that we on the ground have come to regard the killing of bandits as bonus after months of seemingly fruitless activity.*"[48]

With accurate intelligence, the British were able to improve on their bombing accuracy. In one operation, with the help of informants, an insurgent camp was accurately fixed on the ground and bombed from the air. Due to the accurate intelligence, 14 of the 21 insurgents in the camp were killed.[49] Thus it was seen that the success and effectiveness of such operations was hinged on accurate intelligence to fix the target correctly. In the words of Colonel Clutterbuck, "*Every*

*successful bombing operation I know of was the result of a carefully
planned, delicate operation involving an agent. That takes time and
pinpoint accuracy. An agent has always been in on it, it has been an
intelligence type operation.*"[50]

Conclusion

The three main reasons for the defeat of the communist insurgents
were aggressive anti-guerrilla tactics, winning the hearts and minds
of the local population and lack of support from any foreign country.
Air Power played an important role in the anti-guerrilla campaign.

One of the most important roles was in troop mobility and
resupply. Air supply helped the troops remain in the jungle for
greater lengths of time. As analysed by Air Commodore Warcup, *"In
mountainous jungle country the ground forces must have mobility.
I suggest to you this can come only from air support. Without air
mobility, the campaign would have been much more expensive than
it was, and might still be going on today. Mobility was attained by
air supply, helicopters and STOL aircraft.*"[51]

The flexibility of helicopters was also important for evacuating
casualties. They evacuated some 5,000 during the Emergency.
Medical attention was also extended to the Malayan people and helped
in the hearts and mind campaign.

Offensive air support was not a major factor in defeating the
insurgency. It was only useful when accurate intelligence was
available and the insurgents' position was known. However, strafing
and bombing did help in creating a nuisance value and lowering the
morale of the insurgent.

Air power was useful in defeating the insurgency. The main
contribution to the counterinsurgency operations was in the way that
air power was utilised in the indirect roles. From reconnaissance to
aerial mapping, crop-spraying to psychological warfare and from
medical evacuation to deploying troops, the indirect roles of air
power in the Malayan Emergency showed how air power can support
the larger political military effort in a small war. Although clearly
auxiliary to the main military focus on ground operations, the wider

counter-insurgency strategy was aided considerably by the indirect application of air power.

Endnotes

1. Clutterback Richard. The Long War – The Emergency in Malaya 1948-1960. Cassell London, 1966. p-35

2. O'Balance Edgar. Malaya: The Communist Insurgent War, 1948-1960. Faber and Faber Limited, London, 1966. p-82.

3. http://www.nzhistory.net.nz/media/photo/malayan-emergency-map. Last visited on 13 Oct 11.

4. Clutterback. Op.cit. p- 15.

5. O'balance. Op cit. p -76.

6. Comber Leon. The Origins Of The Cold War In Southeast Asia: The Case Of The Communist Party Of Malaya (1948–1960) – A Special Branch Perspective. Kajian Malaysia, Vol. 27, No. 1 & 2, 2009. http://web.usm.my/km/27(1&2),2009/KM%20SE-%20XXVI%20NO%201%20&%202%20ART%202%20(39-59).pdf last accessed on 11 Oct 11. As per this paper, the origins of the 1948–1960 communist uprising in Malaya was a question of debate on whether the decision to start the revolt in June 1948 was part of a global revolutionary movement orchestrated by the Soviet Union as part of the Cold War in Asia, or was it instead arrived at by the MCP based on the local situation in Malaya. The conference did not openly declare for insurrection but its mood was one of extreme belligerence towards colonial rule. The paper goes on to give the views of the Malayan Special Branch. They opined that the Secretary General of the MCP considered that the only way forward was to resort to violence to overthrow the government.

7. Clutterback. Op. cit. p-31.

8. Peterson, Reinhardt and Conger. Symposium on the Role of Air Power in Counterinsurgency and Unconventional Warfare: The Malayan Emergency. The Rand Corporation, Santa Monica California. p- 7. http://www.rand.org/pubs/research_memoranda/2005/RM3651.pdf. Accessed on 14 October 2011.

9. Ibid. p- 9.

10. Clutterback. Op. cit. p-156.

11. http://www.britains-smallwars.com/malaya/aircraft.html#dakota. Accessed on

19 October 2011.

12. The Avro Type 694, better known as the Avro Lincoln, was a British four-engine heavy bomber.

13. Bristol Aeroplane Company's Brigand was a British anti-shipping/ground attack/dive bomber attack aircraft.

14. The Bristol Type 156 Beaufighter, often referred to as simply the Beau, was a British long-range heavy fighter modification of the Bristol Aeroplane Company's earlier Beaufort torpedo bomber design. The name Beaufighter is a portmanteau of "Beaufort" and "fighter".

15. The de Havilland DH.103 Hornet was a piston engine fighter. Entering service at the end of the Second World War, the Hornet equipped post war RAF Fighter Command day fighter units in the UK and was later used successfully as a strike fighter in Malaya.

16. The de Havilland DH.98 Mosquito was a British multi-role combat aircraft that served during the Second World War and the postwar era. It was known affectionately as the "Mossie" to its crews and was also nicknamed "The Wooden Wonder".

17. The de Havilland DH.100 Vampire was a British jet-engine fighter commissioned by the Royal Air Force during the Second World War.

18. The Hawker Tempest was a British fighter aircraftprimarily used by the Royal Air Force (RAF) in the Second World War. The Tempest was an improved derivative of theHawker Typhoon, and one of the most powerful fighter aircraft used during the war.

19. The Gloster Meteor PR Mk.10 was a high level reconnaissance aircraft.

20. The Vickers Valetta was a British twin-engine military transport aircraft.

21. The Short S.25 Sunderland was a British flying boat patrol bomber developed for the Royal Air Force. It was one of the most powerful and widely used flying boats throughout the Second World War.

22. The Douglas DC-3 is an American fixed-wing propeller-driven aircraft whose speed and range revolutionised air transport

23. The Scottish Aviation Pioneer was a Short Take Off and Landing (STOL) aircraft manufactured by Scottish Aviation in Scotland. It was used for casualty evacuation and communications and could accommodate a pilot and up to five passengers.

24. Auster Aircraft Limited was a British aircraft manufacturer from 1938 to 1961.

The aircraft was in a variety of roles such as Air Observation Post (AOP), mail delivery and VIP transport,

25. The Westland WS-51 Dragonfly helicopter was built by Westland Aircraft and was a license-built version of the American Sikorsky S-51. This helicopter was first deployed in Malaya in the reconnaissance, medical evacuation and Search Air Rescue roles.

26. The Westland Whirlwind helicopter was a British licence-built version of the U.S. Sikorsky S-55/H-19 Chickasaw. It was also used in the Search Air Rescue role.

27. The North American F-86 Sabre (sometimes called the Sabrejet) was a transonic jet fighter aircraft.

28. The English Electric Canberra is a first-generation jet-powered light bomber.

29. Peterson, Reinhardt and Conger. op.cit p – 26.

30. Ibid. p- 31.

31. Simpson Gordon. Not by Bombs Alone, Lessons from Malaya. p-96 . http://www.au.af.mil/au/awc/awcgate/jfq/1622.pdf. Accessed on 15 Nov 11.

32. Clutterback. Op. cit. p-159.

33. Villatoux & Catherine. Voices from Heaven. www.psywar.org/voicesfromheaven.php. Assessed on 21 Oct 11.

34. Clutterback. Op. cit. p-160.

35. Simpson. Op. cit.. p-97 .

36. Peterson, Reinhardt and Conger. op.cit p-28.

37. Helicopters in Small Wars. Airpower's Most Important Asset in Irregular Warfare? http://www.scribd.com/doc/50368519/Helicopters-and-Small-Wars-Airpower-s-Most-Important-Asset-in-Irregular-Warfare. Assessed on 24 October 2011.

38. Clutterback. Op. cit. p-157.

39. Peterson, Reinhardt and Conger. op.cit p-35.

40. Miers Richard. Shoot to Kill. London, Faber & Faber 1959. p-159.

41. Great Aviation Quotes. http://www.skygod.com/quotes/predictions.html. Assessed on 24 Oct 11.

42. Boyne J Walter. How the Helicopter Changed Modern Warfare. p- 68. http://

books.google.co.in. Assessed on 24 Oct 11.

43. Miers. Op. cit. p-120.

44. Ibid. pp-117 -118.

45. Simpson. Op. cit. p-97.

46. Malaya 1948-1960. http://www.britains-smallwars.com/malaya/malayan1. html. Assessed on 11 Nov 11.

47. Peterson, Reinhardt and Conger. op.cit p-60

48. Tiwary AK. Air Power and Counterinsurgency. Jammu and Kashmir as a model. Lancer Books New Delhi. p- 69.

49. Clutterback. Op. cit. p-162.

50. Peterson, Reinhardt and Conger. op.cit p-54.

51. Ibid. p-79.

Airpower And Insurgencies - Lessons Learnt

The use of airpower is a political decision.

Clausewitz has described war as, "*a true political instrument, a continuation of political intercourse, carried on with other means.*"[1] General Chang Ting–Chen of Mao Zedong's central committee once stated that revolutionary war was 80 per cent political action and only 20 per cent military.[2] Insurgencies are political in nature as has been brought out earlier. They are armed struggles, aiming to overthrow the legal government in power. To do this, the insurgent has to win over the people and ensure their support. A comprehensive strategy is a pre-requisite in defeating any insurgency. This strategy is not purely military in nature but is a political one. James S Corum and Wray R Johnson, state in their book, "*unsuccessful counterinsurgency campaigns such as the Portuguese operation in Africa, the French in Algeria, the Rhodesian Republic, and the Soviets in Afghanistan were characterised by a strategy that viewed the war almost solely as a military operation and ignored the political and economic dimensions of the conflict.*"[3] In Iraq, the United States fought the insurgents with such a failing strategy that it required to fight with a large conventional force, matching the insurgents man to man and it needed to physically occupy the enemy territory.[4] Col Dennis Drew has brought out that, "*any successful counterinsurgent strategy must incorporate a three-pronged approach.*[5] The government must immediately address the reason of popular unrest; it must identify and obliterate the underground political infrastructure of the insurgent, and must defeat the insurgent military forces. The role that the security and armed forces play in defeating the insurgency is subsidiary to the political goals. Therefore, the extent and roles in which air power is utilised in counterinsurgency operations has to be a part of a larger political strategy.

One of the characteristics of airpower is the ability to apply direct force at almost any given place. Excess use of force can be counterproductive as it could erode the support of the people, who are the centre of gravity of counterinsurgency operations.[6] In today's media savvy world, excessive direct action from the air, resulting in casualties can be blown out of proportions by the media. No political party would accept such adverse publicity. At the same time, the unfavourable publicity would help the insurgent by providing him with a platform for adverse propaganda. If airpower is applied correctly, it can weaken the insurgents' political and strategic position and act as a catalyst in bringing him into the political process.

Insurgencies are waged by the poor against a powerful government. Airpower is seen as a weapon of the strong and powerful. Therefore, there is a tendency for the general population to view the offensive use of airpower against the poor insurgent as cruel and heavy handed. Airpower may be the most appropriate weapon at times to strike at the insurgents' heart, but its use will create a public outcry. This creates confusion in the minds of the politicians on whether to pay a political price on its use or keep national interest in mind. The government has to factor in the political repercussions involved in the use of airpower in the offensive role.

Offensive airpower was used in the Malaya Emergency with the approval of the politicians. As quoted in an article featuring in a book titled Airpower, Insurgency and the "War on Terror", *"Airpower seemed to provide a quick and visible quick fix for the political community frustrated by the invariable gradual progress made by troops on the ground and enabled politicians in London to appease the local politicians and media."* [7] The use of airpower in counterinsurgency operations is purely dependent on the constraints of the political rulers.

An Insurgency, which is mainly a political and not militarily problem, needs to be controlled with political solutions with a minimum cost in terms of money, resources and bloodshed. As far back as in 1920, the British used airpower in subduing insurgencies as it offered them a cheaper solution as compared to utilising the army, and also that there was a loss of fewer lives. This was politically acceptable to a cash strapped Britain. The Governor of Somaliland considered *"that the threats from the air offer the surest guarantee of peace and order in Somaliland."*[8]

Insurgents may also be supported by foreign nations. They may take recourse of taking refuge in neighbouring countries supporting the insurgency. Airpower can be successfully employed in targeting such sanctuaries, or they can be targeted quietly by small ground units. It would be a political decision to escalate the situation by applying airpower thereby sending a strong political signal to the country supporting the insurgency.

Joint Operations

Counterinsurgency operations need to be joined to ensure that airpower is effectively exploited. The role of military forces in fighting any insurgency has to be in support of the larger comprehensive strategy consisting of political, social, economic and security aspects. The military forces are in support of the civil security forces. In turn, the use of airpower has to be in co-ordination with the ground forces, consisting of all agencies involved in counterinsurgency operations. Thus, we can conclude that *"airpower is most effective when it is carefully coordinated with ground forces."*[9]

During the Malaya Emergency, the Director of Operations, General Sir Harold Briggs envisaged the role of the RAF - *"operate in conjunction with and in support of the ground forces. This support may include offensive air strikes; air supply, visual and photographic reconnaissance, survey photography and inter-communication."*[10] The major roles in support of the ground forces were troop mobility and insertion into the insurgency affected areas, casualty evacuation, Command and Control, Cordon and Search operations and resupply of troops.

There is no doubt that ground forces would be able to defeat an insurgency. However, if integrated with the use of airpower, the insurgency would be defeated in a shorter period, with lesser loss of life and with a saving of resources. Airpower can contribute significant support to land forces conducting counterinsurgency operations. Counterinsurgency operations are by nature joint with air and land power, being interdependent on each other.[11]

To be joint operations in the true sense, air operations should be integrated into the plans of the ground forces at the strategic and tactical levels. Ideally speaking, air operations should be integrated at the lowest level of ground formations which will be fighting the insurgents. The smallest unit such as a platoon would be the first to engage with the insurgent. These elements would be the first to request for air support and therefore must be trained and equipped to do so effectively and efficiently. During the Algerian Insurgency, the Tactical Air Command had a very agile control set up. A Company under attack from the insurgents was also able to call up for air support.

In turn, the aircrew must also be exposed to the ground terrain as far as possible to give them a chance to appreciate the requirements of air support in the soldier's perspective. We have seen that this was done during the Malaya Emergency.

Offensive Use of Airpower

In fighting an insurgency, the offensive role of airpower becomes more important when the insurgents have managed to muster and train sufficient forces to stand and fight in a conventional manner. Direct application of airpower against insurgents has been historically most effective when they concentrate in large forces. This situation provides readily identifiable targets for aerial attack. During the Malayan Insurgency, the insurgents were using guerrilla tactics and operating from the jungles. They did not really offer any identifiable targets from the air. The RAF delivered a large tonnage of bombs which resulted in not even 20 insurgents being killed, working out to be a very high ratio of bombs delivered to insurgents killed, a result, not commensurate with the effort.

The overall purpose of offensive air operations is to seize the initiative from the insurgents and keep them under continuous pressure. Offensive air operations should concentrate less on killing guerrilla soldiers (with its inevitable collateral damage and bystander deaths) and more on demonstrating that government forces can go anywhere at any time making insurgents unsafe anywhere. Offensive airpower has a strong deterrent and coercive effect.

When air strikes are to be resorted to, rather than using area weapons, offensive air operations should employ surgical strikes with precision, designed to eliminate insurgents without collateral damage. This would keep the insurgent forces dispersed, preoccupied, distracted, and harassed at every turn. Offensive air strikes in Malaya demoralised the insurgents to a great extent. It also helped them to be flushed out into areas where the security forces were lying in ambush.

If airpower is used to bomb civilians, it may turn out to have an adverse effect on the fight against insurgency. There is a danger of losing popular support due to collateral damage from air attack. Unless the enemy presents an identifiable formation well clear of civilians, the possibility of alienating the populace due to inadvertent injury far outweighs the advantage of striking small irregular groups or units.[12] There are a number of instances in Jammu and Kashmir, where the employment of offensive air power against insurgents could have saved many lives of security forces. An example of one such incident is employment of helicopters in the offensive role for eliminating insurgents hiding in secluded Bakharwal huts in J&K.[13] The insurgents could be identified and located with accuracy and there was no chance of collateral damage.

The French in Algeria used bomber aircraft against villages when the French troops came under attack. Such attacks had an adverse effect destroying schools and causing many civilian casualties. It brought negative publicity to the French and also strengthened the support of the local population towards the insurgents. Unless the enemy presents an identifiable formation well clear of civilians, the possibility of alienating the population due to inadvertent injury far outweighs the advantage of striking small irregular groups or insurgent units. In the words of Gen Stanley Allen McChrystal, the Commander, International Security Assistance Force (ISAF) in 2009-2010, *"From a conventional standpoint, the killing of two insurgents in a group of ten leaves eight remaining: 10-2=8. From the insurgent standpoint, those two killed were likely related to many others who will want vengeance. If civilian casualties occurred, that number will be much higher. Therefore, the death of two creates more willing recruits: 10 minus 2 equals 20 (or more) rather than 8."*[14]

In FATA, the Pakistani Air Force (PAF) carried out more than 5,500 strike sorties from May 2008 onwards.[15] Prior to the operations, numerous reconnaissance missions were flown by F-16 aircraft. These missions were able to detect terrorist training camps, ammunition dumps and command and control facilities.[16] Two days before the ground offensive was launched, the PAF launched a series of interdiction and close air support missions.

The use of direct power by PAF has been considered to be valuable only at the tactical level. Offensive airpower caused significant destruction to the insurgents' strong holds and diminished their ability to influence the local population. At the strategic level, it paid a high cost due to civilian casualties.[17] Primarily due to collateral damage and its psychological effects, the direct use of airpower is attributed to contributing to the deteriorating security in FATA and elsewhere in Pakistan. There is also a feeling that the use of airpower is an important reason as to why the insurgency escalated.[18]

To ensure that there is no collateral damage, rules of engagement must be formulated accordingly and strictly followed. During the military intervention by NATO forces in Libya, in March 2011, the NATO forces utilised air power for targeting command-and-control centres, airfields, supply routes, radar stations and Libya's anti-aircraft defence batteries. During one attack, as the Tornados prepared to launch the Storm Shadow missiles, which have a range of 150 miles, they were instructed not to fire because there were civilians at the target.[19] At no stage should civilian casualties be acceptable.

When offensive airpower is required to be applied, the best weapons to be used are precision weapons and weapons that minimize collateral damage by reduced blast effect. In counterinsurgency operations, the use of excessive force can destroy the legitimacy and support for an operation. The greater the number of civilian casualties/deaths or extent of damage to civilian infrastructure such as water, electricity, transportation, etc. the greater is the adverse effect on the counterinsurgency campaign. The aim of offensive action in conventional war is to impose one's will over the adversary. In counterinsurgency operations, imposing the government's will by offensive action, on the insurgents is required at the tactical level. Injury to the civil population and other collateral damage will have an adverse strategic effect which the insurgents will exploit, setting back months of building rapport and forging trusting relationships with the population. Due to this, there is a requirement to balance the amount of force applied, ensuring minimum collateral damage and at the same time maximum effect on the insurgent. Thus the requirement to use weapons which result in minimum collateral damage is critical in counterinsurgency operations. Small Diameter Bombs (SDB) such as the GBU-39 are available and have been used in situations where the risk of collateral damage was high. The SDM, developed by Boeing is described as the next generation low-cost and low collateral-damage precision strike weapon.[20] In Afghanistan, Coalition Forces used inert concrete filled, precision, GBU-12 bombs to destroy selected targets without the blast effects of a live weapon.[21] Other variants of such SDBs are the Focused Lethality Munitions (FLM). Rather than a steel casing that hurls deadly fragments several hundred feet in each direction, the FLM has a carbon-fibre casing that disintegrates into harmless dust. In addition, the explosive filler is mixed with small tungsten particles that slow down rapidly due to air friction. This creates a concentrated zone of destruction just a few meters across, with little damage outside that radius.[22] To ensure that smart weapons hit the right target, operators need to know the location of the right target. This has been made possible with persistent surveillance and reconnaissance capabilities. Modern sensors such as Unmanned Air Vehicles (UAVs) have the capability to loiter over an area of interest for long durations with their sensors having the ability to discern targets.

Strategic Bombing

Strategic bombing is a method of attacking an adversary's centres of gravity to produce a level of destruction and disintegration of an enemy's military capacity to a point where the enemy is no longer capable of carrying out aggressive activity.

Insurgencies do not lend themselves to the more strategic roles of air power and the use of immense fire power such as strategic bombing. Strategic bombing is a military strategy used in a war situation between nation states with the goal of defeating an enemy nation-state by destroying its economic ability and public will, to wage war rather than destroying its defence forces. Insurgencies lack large transportation, communications, or military targets which can easily be targeted from the air. They operate using guerrilla tactics, exploiting their inherent advantage of initiative, surprise and mobility. They blend with the population, making it difficult to identify them. Thus they offer no worthwhile target for strategic bombing.

Strategic bombing may be acceptable to politicians who are waging or supporting a counterinsurgency campaign on foreign soil. It would meet the requirements of providing a highly visible and quick response to the problem, without the danger of own casualties which are unacceptable.

Close Air Support

One of the effective roles of offensive air action is in providing close air support to the ground forces engaged in skirmishes with insurgents. It is one of the most beneficial ways of utilising offensive air power by its ability to provide responsive fire power with a high degree of precision. In Algeria, the French were able to call upon airpower in close air support missions very effectively. This was possible due to a very efficient communication system between the troops, the Tactical Air Centre and the aircraft, enabling the troops on the ground to demand for immediate air support and receive fire support from the air, thereby neutralising the insurgents. Command and control of the situation switched between the lead helicopter and the ground forces and vice versa as per requirement. The system was fluid, efficient, and successful. This capability gave French forces a tremendous advantage.

Pre-Planned Close Air Support

When Close Air Support is pre-planned and dove tailed into the ground operations, it has the advantage of being fully integrated into the battle plan. The area of interest is known in advance, target - weapon matching can be carried out and air power assets can be planned to respond to numerous contingencies. This detailed planning would ensure that offensive fire power is carried out with maximum effectiveness and efficiency, at the same time guaranteeing minimum collateral damage and fratricide.

In a bid to minimise collateral damage to innocent civilians, security forces should endeavour to steer the insurgents away from the local population. A pre-requisite would be support of the local population and sufficient security forces. Once the insurgents are physically isolated, airpower's precision and firepower may be able to be applied surgically. Such an approach would allow pre-planned close air support to be gainfully employed.

Immediate Close Air Support

Immediate Close Air Support has its drawbacks, primarily, as it is unplanned. Aircrew and ground controllers would not be able to study the target in advance, nor would correct target –weapon matching be carried out. An Aircraft for such immediate air support may not be available. Though airpower would be able to deliver offensive fire support and assist the besieged ground forces, the probability of collateral damage and fratricide increases.

On the whole, when utilising airpower in the offensive role in counterinsurgency operations, Close Air Support, especially pre-planned missions, plays an important part in defeating the insurgency. The ability to provide rapid and precise fire power permits the ground forces to operate in a more dispersed manner, which is desirable in counterinsurgency operations. Aircrew who would have been brought into the targeting loop would be in a better position to locate and identify the target correctly from the air, ensuring minimal collateral damage.

Other than the surveillance and reconnaissance roles, the UAV has the capability of being armed and utilised in the offensive role. Armed UAVs have been used extensively in counterinsurgency operations by the Americans in Afghanistan. The MQ-1 "Predator" and the MQ-9 "Reaper" have been successfully employed for close air support (CAS) missions. In the CAS role, Forward Air Controllers (FACs) communicate with remotely located UAV operators, guiding them in releasing weapons in the close vicinity of friendly troops.

These UAVs are officially designated "Armed, Multi-mission, Medium-altitude, Long endurance, Remotely Piloted Aircraft."[23] An important characteristic of the Predator and Reaper UAVs is the ability to loiter for extended periods, in some cases for more than 24 hours. This ability to loiter is very important and these UAVs are able to do the job of a number of such platforms which would otherwise be required for 24 hours surveillance. Operating higher than helicopters and with a lower signature than manned, jet-powered fighter aircraft, the Predator or Reaper UAVs are neither visible nor audible. This in turn has an indirect psychological effect where potential targets would need to assume that an armed UAV could be orbiting within striking distance at all times.

Interdiction

The logistic structure in insurgencies is usually different from those of a conventional army. They rely on the local population for their daily requirements of sustenance. The lines of communication such as roads and bridges are used by both the insurgents and the civil population. Hence, they do not have well defined lines of communication which may be interdicted, without any detrimental effects to the overall counterinsurgency campaign.

When an insurgency is at its peak and the insurgent forces have been able to muster an army, air interdiction may have to be carried out to disrupt the supply lines. These supply lines need not be limited to land routes but may also emanate from the sea. Smuggling in arms and ammunition, drugs and other banned articles, to finance and support the insurgency, by the sea, is a convenient method of transportation.

Targeting

Airpower can be projected over large distances with accuracy. Precision ammunition has improved the levels of accuracy and continuous ISR has been able to locate obscure targets, accurately fixing their position for being targeted with precision. Political leadership is very important for an insurgency to succeed. This leadership provides vision, direction, guidance, coordination, and organisational harmony to the insurgency. There would be other key individuals which play vital roles in the insurgency such as planning, military training and co-ordinating operations. Targeting these individuals with the use of airpower is viable.

Troop Mobility

Rough terrain and poor surface connectivity can be serious impediments to counter insurgency operations, while they are advantageous to the insurgents. The insurgents follow guerilla tactics, taking the initiative to attack security forces at their choice of place and time. They will ambush the patrolling security forces in isolated areas, and then disappear before reinforcements arrive. Airpower helps overcome these obstacles. This was successfully experienced by the British in Malaya where helicopters transported troops directly into the area of interest and thus saving them from long marches through thick jungles.

An important troop deployment operations the RAF carried out during the Malayan Emergency was the insertion of the Special Air Service (SAS) troops. These missions were critical to the overall strategic requirement of reducing the paramilitary capabilities of the enemy. Elite SAS units were only able to endure stealthy patrols for long periods in the deep jungle and to hunt down and attack insurgent camps by being deployed and resupplied from the air.

In Algeria, an important lesson learnt by the French was that any movement of ground forces by surface transport was immediately detected by the insurgents. Therefore, all transport movement was stopped by the army before any operation. Troops would be inserted by helicopters directly into the area of interest. Prior to arriving, the area would be softened by aerial bombardment by fixed wing aircraft. Precisely two minutes after this bombardment, the helicopters would arrive, disgorging troops. Helicopters would also give the troops and helicopters disembarking troops, covering fire.

Casualty Evacuation

Helicopters are capable of landing in small clearings and evacuate battle casualties or hover to winch up casualties where no suitable landing area exists. This is a great morale booster to the ground forces.

To wounded soldiers, the knowledge that a smooth ride in a helicopter to hospital is assured instead of a journey through the jungles or tough terrain on a stretcher gives them tremendous confidence about their survivability and uplifts their morale. A corollary to this is that such injuries would not divert manpower towards tending to the injured and as a result not hamper operations.

The vital indirect roles of airpower - troop mobility resupply and Cas Evac, are crucial in aiding security forces in fighting insurgents by negating the need for difficult and gruelling treks through thick jungles and providing them with an element of surprise, and by enabling those patrols to maximise their endurance by sustaining their medical and logistic requirements.

Air Power helps in Reducing Force Levels

With the judicious application of airpower in the ISR, troop mobility, logistic supply, casualty evacuation and offensive support roles, the counterinsurgent to insurgent force ratios can be reduced to a great extent.[24] As seen in past insurgencies, counterinsurgent to insurgent force ratios can vary from 10, as in Algeria to 50 as in Jammu and Kashmir.[25] During the Malay Emergency, where the force ratio was 12,[26] it was estimated that without the use of helicopters, four times the number of ground troops would have been required to fight the insurgency.[27]

Counterinsurgency operations are manpower intensive. Airpower, when used to transport troops and in other administrative duties, provides numerous advantages.

- Troop movement by air enables the ground forces to avoid moving by roads which are vulnerable to being mined or the troops ambushed. By moving the troops by air, it does away with the requirement of protecting these troop convoys with a significant number of troops. This in turn frees troops from such secondary duties and permits them to be deployed in counterinsurgency operations – resulting in an overall reduction of forces.

- Transporting troops by air denies the insurgent with a lucrative target and an opportunity for adverse propaganda for the government.

- Airborne logistic supply hastens resupply of troops in the field, enabling them to move lighter resulting in more incessant ground operations.

- By doing away with resupplying the troops by road, the chances of losing the supplies to insurgent ambushes also reduces, resulting in reducing the amount of redundant supplies and man hours that must be used for pushing supplies into the system for catering for losses. This also acts to the disadvantage of the insurgent who may depend upon captured government logistic supplies to sustain him.

Intelligence, Surveillance, Reconnaissance

Employing the medium of air provides a highly capable method of obtaining intelligence. In the early history of airpower, balloons and aircraft were used as aerial observation platforms for observing and directing artillery fire and gathering intelligence. Obtaining intelligence is very important to the success of counterinsurgency operations. Airpower provides a very efficient collection method. The ability of airpower to provide opportune, wide area surveillance and reconnaissance in counterinsurgency operations remains vital to the chances of their success. Aerial surveillance and reconnaissance makes it difficult for the insurgents to shift to conventional tactics and carry out attacks at their will.

The role of intelligence in counter-insurgency is essentially different from intelligence in conventional war. The primary mission of intelligence gathering in conventional wars is locating the enemy's forces and order of battle. With the advent of modern technology, this is relatively an easier task as compared to intelligence gathering in counterinsurgency operations. In conventional wars, high end technological assets such as space and Signal Intelligence (SIGINT) are utilised in intelligence gathering. In counter-insurgency operations, one of the basic requirements is first to understand the nature and reasons for the insurgency and thereafter monitor the insurgent organisation. This implies collecting and collating information about the whole society, understanding local conditions, observing public opinion, and utilising Human Intelligence (HUMINT) assets to penetrate the insurgent organisation to provide inputs regarding its force disposition. The inputs that need to be collected do not have large signatures to observe or lasting signals to intercept and to add to this, the insurgents conceal themselves within the local population.

Intelligence, Surveillance and Reconnaissance (ISR) can be defined as "*activity that synchronises and integrates the planning and operation of sensors, assets, and processing, exploitation, and dissemination systems in direct support of current and future operations.*"[28] In ISR, Surveillance and reconnaissance refer to the means by which the information is monitored. Surveillance is defined as "*systematic observation of air and space, surface or substance, or subsurface areas over a period of time by visual, aerial, electronic, photographic or other means.*" Reconnaissance is defined as, "*a mission undertaken to obtain, by visual observation or other detection methods, information about the activities and resources of an enemy or potential enemy or to secure data concerning meteorological, hydrographical or geographic characteristics of a particular area.*" Surveillance is a continuous process carried out over a considerable period of time. On the other hand, reconnaissance can be explained as mission specific, carried out for a specific purpose. Intelligence is the objective of ISR, and surveillance and reconnaissance are carried out to contribute to that objective.

ISR operations must be aimed at providing relevant, accurate and timely intelligence to the organisation for planning and conducting counterinsurgency operations. ISR for counterinsurgency operations includes all intelligence disciplines, all sources of information, and all aspects of the process of collecting data and turning it into operationally useful intelligence upon which decisions and actions can be based.

Conventional operations or counter terrorist operations generally require a more simple approach to intelligence than counterinsurgency operations. In conventional or counter terrorist operations, it is important to identify the target, fix the target with precise coordinates and use an appropriate weapon to neutralise it. ISR missions should not be limited to locating and assisting in neutralising insurgent organisations by offensive action. They must also be gainfully utilised in trying to understand the behaviour of individuals, groups and the population to assess behavioural changes as the counterinsurgency operations develop. This patterns of life development is an intelligence intensive effort. Furthermore, the range of intelligence needed to be effective is comparatively wider for COIN, including intelligence dependent on cultural factors that cannot be provided by airborne sensors alone. In counterinsurgency operations, ISR does not have an identifiable end point in terms of data collection.

Intelligence gathered by aerial platforms can give you a great amount of data. It can observe the pattern of life and discern any changes in such routine patterns. However, it cannot give answers to the reasons for the changes. Counterinsurgency operations are dependent on effective intelligence, which can be analysed only by individuals who are familiar with the ground situation and also have sufficient operational experience in fighting the insurgency. Intelligence gathered through air assets must be quickly routed for timely analysis to a joint intelligence centre. This centre would build a picture by painting in intelligence inputs from other sources such as HUMINT. The availability of actionable intelligence to the field is hastened by the combination of gathering data through aerial assets and ground based assets and analysis by experienced individuals. This was also experienced in El Salvador, which fought a protracted insurgency from 1980 to 1992. Only after an Intelligence Centre was set up for counterinsurgency operations, were the government forces able to integrate intelligence inputs from various sources, leading to an improvement in their combat capabilities.[29]

The government forces must utilise all the available assets for gathering intelligence. Airpower resources in most cases will not face a high threat environment in counterinsurgency operations. Therefore, although expensive, high-tech equipment such as airborne warning and control system (AWACS) and satellites will remain indispensable in conventional wars, the requirement to preserve these valuable assets and at the same time limit the costs of counterinsurgency operations may influence the employment of lower-technology equipment whenever possible. Light and slow moving civilian aircraft can be effectively used for aerial surveillance and reconnaissance.

With the advent of Unmanned Air Vehicles (UAVs), airborne surveillance has become more effective. Modern UAV platforms have the ability to stay airborne for long durations. They are equipped with state of the art surveillance equipment that has the capability to provide real time and clear imagery of large areas to remote ground stations. These platforms can operate over areas of interest unobtrusively and persistently. Thus they are ideally suited in the ISR role for counterinsurgency operations. Loren Thompson, a military analyst at the Lexington Institute in USA remarked, "*Unmanned vehicles present a whole new dimension to detecting and destroying of terrorists' cells. It's almost like having your own little satellite over a terrorist cell.*"[30] With the ability to provide 24 hour surveillance, ISR capabilities are able to establish a pattern of life more effectively than inputs from ground based sources, as experienced by American forces in Iraq and Afghanistan.[31] Continuous airborne surveillance of insurgency infested areas, when combined with other sources of intelligence, increases the possibility and probability for security forces to take the initiative from the insurgents. Correct and timely intelligence is important in targeting from the air. Precision weapons may put the weapon on the target, but intelligence can tell which target is the right one.

UAVs can support paramilitary patrols by flying ahead to detect possible threats. Once detected, the ground force can manoeuvre around the threat or call in air or other fire support against it. Airborne surveillance can also monitor the likely escape routes that the insurgents will take and guide the security forces accordingly. Airborne surveillance of economic and communication targets such as oil pipelines and roads are a very cost effective way of ensuring their protection from insurgent attacks and sabotage. The United States had created a Task Force in Iraq code named ODIN, which stands for Observe, Detect, Identify and Neutralise, specifically for reconnaissance, surveillance, targeting and acquisition. The concept employed Army aviation assets such as helicopters and UAVs, to maintain a constant watch for enemies placing bombs or improvised explosive devices (IEDs) on Iraq's roads.[32] This ability affords unprecedented situational awareness and physical presence over the insurgency affected areas.

With the availability of different payloads, UAV's have the ability to monitor communication made on the airways via mobile / satellite phones, R/T or otherwise. Counterterrorism or counterinsurgency targets in areas where UAVs operate must work under tight communications discipline and constraints. Monitoring conversation not only provides intelligence inputs, it can also pinpoint their location and be a cause of an immediate or potentially lethal attack. The UAVs ability to gather intelligence by monitoring conversation not only affects the leaders of the insurgency but also their entire organisations. Unrestrained conversation can yield lethal results. The natural response to such situations would be to lay down security protocols and restrict or stop open conversation, especially with untrusted individuals. When the intricacies of security protocols become important to the insurgent, the positive fallout for the security forces is in the insurgents' restricting their operations. Such intelligence gathering methods can also sow distrust within the organisation ultimately increasing distrust amongst individuals. This would diminish the ability for achieving the objectives of the insurgency.

The Los Angeles Times reported in April 2008 that in Afghanistan NATO "forces recently have had unusual success in tracking and targeting mid-level Taliban field commanders, killing scores of them in pinpoint airstrikes."[33] The Taliban believed that they were being targeted by monitoring their cell phone signals.

Psychological Effects of Air Power

In the fight against an insurgency, in order to reduce or destroy the insurgents' military ability to wage the insurgency, there will be two effects - the physical and the psychological. The physical aspects are the perceptible ones like physical destruction of insurgents, their equipment and training camps and other viable targets. However, the psychological aspects are the more indiscernible ones in which targeting instead of winning the insurgents 'hearts and minds' of the insurgents is the main concern. The desired outcome of the psychological campaign is to target the insurgent's mind and render his forces reluctant or unwilling to continue with the insurgency. Degradation or destruction of the insurgents' resolve to continue fighting has a similar effect on its combat capability as actually degrading or destroying its perceivable assets. Hitting the insurgents' critical vulnerabilities for both physical and psychological effect can produce a synergistic outcome on the insurgents' capacity to continue waging the insurgency.

The role of the security forces in combatting insurgencies is very important. They must establish an image that they are invincible and destroy the insurgents' confidence in continuing the insurgency by spreading a feeling of defeat. Simultaneously, the security forces need to integrate psychological operations with 'Winning the Hearts and Minds' of the local population.

Stress and fear are present whenever anyone takes to arms, be it for any cause. 68 per cent of combatants in World War II "admitted that not only had they experienced fear and anxiety at some time during combat, but also that they had experienced it at a level that prevented them from completing their duties."[34] At least fourteen stressors have been identified which include noise, fatigue and lack of sleep.[35] One of airpower's important characteristics of shock effect, when used offensively can produce all these three psychological stressors. Shock effect can also cause confusion in the minds of those targeted resulting in psychological disorientation and degradation of his combat effectiveness. This is possible as airpower can deliver firepower with complete surprise.

It must be noted that these psychological effects of airpower will only be visible when a decision has been taken to use airpower offensively. In a study done by the Rand Corporation, "in the conflict situation in which the enemy troops were not subject to sustained, effective attacks, their resistance did not collapse and they did not surrender or desert en masse."[36]

Offensive airpower is also characterised with the ability to be applied with persistence and precision. Persistence is achieved by continuous surveillance and reconnaissance, while precision is achieved by smart weapons knowing what to hit and where, a by-product of ISR. This not only degrades the physical ability of the insurgent to be violent, but it can also create psychological effects upon insurgents. Airpower can unnerve even the fiercest fighters. In Afghanistan, airpower has been used extensively in targeting the Taliban. Death per se does not extinguish the will to fight in such opponents; rather, it is the hopelessness that arises from the inevitability of death from a source they cannot fight. As one Afghan told The New York Times, "*We pray to Allah that we have American soldiers to kill*" but added pessimistically that "*these bombs from the sky we cannot fight.*"[37] In Iraq, the sound of aircraft is associated with "my buddy getting killed".[38] The association of aerial noise followed by bombing causing death can have a profound psychological effect. This effect can be exploited at times by a show of aerial force when aircraft operate overhead a troubled spot and not by actually carrying out attacks. The very presence of aircraft over head may result in insurgents keeping their heads down, as was seen in Iraq during the two battles of Fallujah in 2004.[39]

Offensive airpower can also create a sense of helplessness in the minds of insurgents' and be a catalyst in making them desert. For example, in Colombia which is ravaged with internal conflict, the rebel group known as the Revolutionary Armed Force of Colombia (FARC is the Spanish acronym) faced numerous desertions, which may result in the insurgency collapsing. According to interviews with former rebels, "the sheer terror of being bombed by Colombian fighter planes" was a crucial factor in their decision to desert.[40] As per a study carried out by the Rand Corporation, sustained effective air attacks demoralised troops to such an extent that it caused many Iraqi soldiers to desert during the Gulf war.[41] To exploit the psychological effects of low morale, willingness to desert and degraded combat effectiveness, mopping up operations by security forces should closely follow the air operations.[42] This was seen in Iraq, during the 100 hour long Coalition Forces ground campaign, which effectively exploited the demoralisation of the Iraqi troops caused by the air campaign.

Troops experiencing the shortage of food has also been identified as one of the stressors during war like situations, especially when compounded with being subjected to other stressors as previously brought out. During the Malayan Emergency, the British endeavoured to deny the insurgents with the availability of food by spraying their crops from the air. Food denial can also be achieved by disrupting the insurgents' lines of communication and interdicting their food supplies. During the Gulf War, many prisoners and deserters cited the shortage of food as one of the reasons for low morale.[43]

To maximise the psychological effects of airpower, Psychological Operations (PSYOPS) need to be also integrated into counterinsurgency operations. PYSOP leaflets can be dropped over a wide area from the air, ensuring that they are well distributed. The leaflets should bring out the advantages of surrendering to government forces and the futility of continuing with the insurgency.[44] On 17 January 1991, Coalition Forces commenced a 38 day aerial offensive on Iraq. Not only was it effective in terms of physical destruction, it was overwhelmingly effective in terms of its psychological impact on deployed Iraqi forces. The paralysing fear and sense of complete defencelessness of troops subjected to B-52 strikes were often magnified by PSYOP leaflets dropped before and after bombing raids, first informing the Iraqis that they were going to be bombed and thereafter, the bombing would be repeated after 24 hours. Their only option was to leave their equipment and desert. "Walk toward Mecca," the leaflets advised.[45]

While planning for counterinsurgency operations, planners must understand that other than the physical destruction, the psychological effects of the counterinsurgency campaign need to be factored in from planning to the conduct of such operations. This would be achievable if experts on psychological operations are included at the planning stage of such operations. The psychological effects will only be visible when the insurgents come under attack from sustained aerial or ground firepower. Demoralising insurgents must be one of the objectives of offensive air operations and not an unplanned dividend.

PSYOP messages help in reinforcing the psychological effects of offensive firepower, by explaining the inevitability of defeat. Such messages cost little but can be a significant force multiplier. PSYOP messages also help in addressing the two fears of surrender, firstly, how to surrender or desert safely and secondly, how the insurgents will be treated after they surrender.

There is also a requirement to assess the psychological impact of airpower. Akin to "battle damage assessment", the impairment of the insurgent's combat capability due to fear, demoralisation, and other non-physical effects brought about by the application of airpower, need to be analysed for refining the areas where airpower may be applied. This would be possible by interrogating insurgents who are captured or who are deserters.

The psychological effects of offensive operations on the local population, which is detrimental to counterinsurgency operations, must be minimised. Civilian casualties must be avoided at all cost, as the innocent civil population is the centre of gravity of any counterinsurgency campaign. Their support has to be won over and not lost by collateral damage from aerial attack. This would depict the government in poor light for using excessive force against innocent civilians.

Other than creating a feeling of despondency and lowering the morale of the insurgent, airpower can be used gainfully in creating a feeling of security in the minds of the local population and depicting the security forces as a competent and efficient force with a humane face. Airpower can be integrated into 'Winning the Hearts and Minds' campaign. A very effective method of winning the hearts and minds of the insurgency effected local population and their support in the fight against insurgency, is by employing air transport to airlift or drop food and medical supplies to citizens living in isolated areas. Another important role would be to bring governance to the doorstep of remote villages not well connected by road, by conveying civil government functionaries to oversee local administration and development.

Endnotes

1   Clausewitz Von Carl. On War. Edited and translated by Howard Mitchel and
     Paret Peter. Princetown University Press. p-87.

2   The US Army and Marine Corps Counterinsurgency Field Manual. p-35. http://
     freeinfosociety.com/media/pdf/3095.pdf. Assessed on 13 March 2012.

3   Corum S Johnson & Johnson R Wray. Air Power in Small Wars. Fighting
     Insurgents and Terrorists. University Press of Kansas. pp- 425 -426

4   Meilinger S Philip. Counterinsurgency From Above. Air Force Magzine.

com. July 2008. Vol 91, No 7. www.airforcemagzine.com/magzineArchives/ Pages/2008/July%202008/0708COIN.aspx Assessed on 13 March 2012.

5   Drew Dennis . Insurgencies and Counterinsurgencies, http://www.au.af.mil/ au/awc/awcgate/cadre/au-ari-cp-88-1.pdf. p-22. Assessed on 21 Nov 11.

6   Counterinsurgency, FM 3-24. Headquarters Department of the US Army, December 2006. p-E-2.

7   Munford Andrew and Kennedy-Pipe Croline. Unnecessary or Unsung? The Strategic Role of Airpower in Britain's Colonial Counter-Insurgency, in Airpower, Insurgency and the "War on Terror", edited by Joel Hayward. RAF Centre for Airpower Studies. p-71.

8   Towle A Philip. Pilots and Rebels. Brassey's UK. p-12.

9   Corum. Op.cit.p- 433.

10   Munford Andrew and Kennedy-Pipe Croline. Unnecessary or Unsung? The Strategic Role of Airpower in Britain's Colonial Counter-Insurgency, in Airpower, Insurgency and the "War on Terror", edited by Joel Hayward. RAF Centre for Airpower Studies. p-70.

11   Counterinsurgency, FM 3-24. Headquarters Department of the US Army, December 2006. p-E-1.

12   Corum Jamesand Johnson Ray. Airpower in Small Wars. Kansas University Press. p- 427-29.

13   Subramanium Arjun. Air Power and Irergular Warfare in the Indian Context. Indian Defence Review. Issue Vol. 24.1, Jan-Mar 2009. www. indiandefencereview.com. Assessed on 22 Nov 11. Bakharwal is a nomadic tribe found in the Himalayas. They use these huts during the summers and abandon them during winter months. In Kashmir, these huts are at times used by the insurgents/terrorists for hiding.

14   Report of the Defence Science Board Task Force on Defence Intelligence. Cointerinsurgency, Intelligence, Surveillance and Reconnaisance Operations. p-39.

15   The Express Tribune. 14 November 2001. http://tribune.com.pk/story/291762/ paf-conducted-5500-bombing-runs-in-fata-since-2008/. Assessed on 23 February 2012.

16   Ibid.

17   Ahmad Irfan. Role of Airpower for Counterinsurgency in Afghanistan and FATA (Federally Administered Tribal Areas). Naval Post Graduate School.

California. pp-82-83

18   Ahmad. Ibid. p-83.

19   Mail Online. 22 March 2011. http://www.dailymail.co.uk/news/article-1368626/ Libya-RAF-abort-attack-SAS-spot-Gaddafi-using-human-shields.html. Assessed on 23 Nov 2011.

20   http://www.boeing.com/defense-space/missiles/sdb/docs/SDB_overview.pdf. Assessed on 05 March 2012.

21   Haendschke Ernie. Adding Less-Lethal Arrows to the Quiver for Counterinsurgency Air Operations. http://www.airpower.au.af.mil/ airchronicles/apj/apj08/sum08/haendschke.html. Assessed on 05 March 2012.

22   http://www.popularmechanics.com/technology/military/planes-uavs/5-weapons-systems-to-reduce-collateral-damage-gbu-39b-focused-lethality-munition#slide-2. Assessed on 05 March 2012.

23   http://www.stratfor.com/weekly/armed-uav-operations-10-years. Assessed on 15 February 2012.

24   Op.cit. Corum. p-435

25   Rabasa Angel, Warner Lesley Anne, Chalk Peter, Khilko Ivan and Shukla Paraag. Money in the Bank- Lessons Learnt from Past Counterinsurgency Operations. Rand Corporation. p-xiv. http://www.rand.org/pubs/occasional_ papers/2007/RAND_OP-185.pdf. Assessed on 04 January 2012.

26   Goode Steven M. A Historical Basis for Force Requirements in Counterinsurgency. p-51. http://www.carlisle.army.mil/usawc/parameters/ Articles/09winter/goode.pdf. Assessed on 11 January 2012.

27   Peterson, Reinhardt and Conger. Op. cit. p- 72.

28   Report of the US Defence Science Board Task Force on Intelligence. Counterinsurgency, Intelligence surveillance and Reconnaissance Operations.p-24.

29   Corum. Op. cit. p- 345.

30   Brook Tom Vanden. Air Force Seeks More Fighter Drones.USA Today.06 March 2008.http://www.usatoday.com/news/washington/2008-03-05-Reapers_N.htm. Assessed on 23 January 2012.

31   Mulrine Anna. A Look Inside the Air Force's Control Center for Iraq and Afghanistan. US News. 29 May 2008. http://www.usnews.com/news/world/ articles/2008/05/29/a-look-inside-the-air-forces-control-center-for-iraq-and-

afghanistan?page=2. Assessed on 23 January 2012. This article describes the operations at an Air Force Control Centre and how UAVs are being used effectively in identifying and tracking insurgent groups.

32   Matthew Cox and Gina Cavallaro: Petraeus: ISR gear is key to success: Army Times. Friday Apr 11 2008 http://www.armytimes.com/news/2008/04/ military_petraeus_gear_042108/. Assessed on 25 January 2012.

33   King Laura. Taliban's New Strategy in Pushing the Wrong Buttons. Los Angeles Times. 23 April 2008. http://articles.latimes.com/2008/apr/23/world/ fg-cellphones23. Assessed on 02 March 2012.

34   Lambert APN. The Psychology of Air Power. London: Royal United Services Institute of Defence Studies. p-39.

35   Ibid.pp-36-39.

36   Hosmer T Stephen. Psychological Effects of US Air Operations in Four Wars 1941-1991. Rand Corporation. p-xxiv.

37   Barry Bearak, "A Nation Challenged: Death on the Ground," The New York Times, 13 October 2001. As quoted in Making Revolutionary Change: Airpower in COIN Today by Dunlop Charles.p-59.

38   Up in the Sky an Unblinking Eye. The Daily Beast. 31 May 2008. http://www. thedailybeast.com/newsweek/2008/05/31/up-in-the-sky-an-unblinking-eye. html. Assessed on 29 February 2012.

39   Armed UAV Operations 10 Years On. Stratfor Global Intelligence. 12 January 2012. http://www.stratfor.com/weekly/armed-uav-operations-10-years. Assessed on 02 March 2012.

40   Forero Juan. Colombia's Rebels Face Possibility of Implosion. Chief Threat Not Deaths, but desertion. Washington Post. 22 March 2008. http://www. washingtonpost.com/wp-dyn/content/article/2008/03/21/AR2008032103536_ pf.html. Assessed on 01 March 2012.

41   Hosmer. Ibid p-xxvi.

42   Bruce A. Lindblom. Psychological Impact of Airpower. p-15. http://www. dtic.mil/cgi-bin/GetTRDoc?AD=ADA351576. Assessed on 29 February 2012.

43   Hosmer. Ibid p-xxvii.

44   Hosmer. Ibid p-xxiii.

45   Lambert. Ibid.pp-63-64.

The Maoist Insurgency

A Short History

The Maoist insurgency draws its name from a brand of Communist radical ideology based on the political ideas of Mao Tse Tung. This insurgency in India can be traced back to the Telangana struggle. Telangana is the eastern part of the former princely state of Hyderabad. Any study on the Maoist Insurgency in India cannot ignore the importance of the rise and fall of the Telangana Movement (1946-51). Telangana is remembered by the Indian Communists as a notable period in the history of peasant struggles for Indian communists. It was the first serious effort by sections of the communist party to understand and learn from the experiences of the Chinese revolution and to develop a comprehensive line for India's democratic revolution.

The movement started when oppressed peasants revolted against the atrocities of their landlord in Jangaon Taluka. The landlord, Visnuru Ramachandra Reddy had been prevented by the peasants from seizing the lands of a lowly washerwoman. On the 04 July 1946, a group of people marched towards the landlord's house, where their leader was killed by the landlord's henchmen. Not in keeping with their normal behaviour of submission, the enraged peasants, swelling to a mob of over 2,000, charged towards the landlord's house, surrounded it,baying for Visnuru Ramachandra Reddy's blood. This was the starting of the Telanganna struggle.[1] This struggle or movement had three lines of thought. The first one drew inspiration from the teachings of Stalin, denouncing Mao. The second one was influenced profoundly by the methods of Mao Tse Tung. The third group was more central in their thinking and professed a parliamentary democratic approach.[2]

This movement was supported by 2000 to 3000 villages, where peasant rule was established. To defend this rule, there was a guerrilla army of 2000 regulars and over 10,000 supporters.[3] The movement was brought under control by the Indian army which marched in to the State of Hyderabad with the intention to merge it into the greater state of India.

In 1957, the Communists succeeded in forming a government in Kerala, which was subsequently overthrown. After the Indo - China war, the Communist party split into two, namely, the Communist Party of India (CPI) and Communist Party of India (Marxist) (CPI [M]). While the CPI professed a theory of 'peaceful road to non-capitalist development', the CPI (M) adopted the centrist line. Though there were serious differences on ideological and tactical grounds, both the parties went ahead with their parliamentary exercises and formed the United Front government in West Bengal.

The next phase of the Maoist Insurgency was seen in West Bengal in the small village of Naxalbari, neighbouring the Indian borders of Nepal. The trigger for the Naxalite Movement, the name of which is derived from the village, was once again a land related bone of contention. A tribal, having obtained a judicial order, went to plough his land on 02 March 1967. The local landlords attacked him with the assistance of their henchmen. The villagers of the area retaliated and started forcefully recapturing their lands. What followed was a rebellion, which left one police sub inspector and nine tribals dead. Within a short span of about two months, this incident acquired great visibility and tremendous support from cross sections of Communist revolutionaries belonging to the state units of the CPI (M) in West Bengal, Bihar, Orissa, Andhra Pradesh, Tamil Nadu, Kerala, Uttar Pradesh and Jammu and Kashmir. The Communist Party of India (Marxist) initiated a violent and bloody uprising in Bengal. One of its leaders, Charu Mazumdar was influenced by the teachings of Mao. He encouraged the peasants and lower class tribals to overthrow the government and upper classes by force. The United Front Government of West Bengal, headed by the CPI (M) was able to contain the insurgency within a short span of 72 days with all the harshest measures possible. The state police collaborated with a strong intelligence network and were able to track the movements of the leaders. The Naxalite Movement in West Bengal culminated with Op Steeple Chase (July 1971), a joint police and military operation.[4]

This movement was an expression of the anger of the poor farmers of West Bengal due to the lack of land reforms. After this movement, West Bengal devised a plan to address the issue of land reforms, which resulted in the movement subsiding.

The 1980s saw the resurgence of Naxal violence in Andhra Pradesh in the manifestation of the Peoples War Group (PWG). This group was officially designated the epithet of Communist Party of India—Marxist Leninist (People's War) was formed on Lenin's birth anniversary on 22 April 1980. By the early 1990s, this movement also proliferated to Orissa, Bihar, Maharashtra and Madhya Pradesh. The aggrandizement of militarisation became the characteristic feature of the PWG. The formation of People's Guerrilla Army (PGA), special guerrilla squads, Permanent Action Team (PAT) and Special Action Team (SAT) were the distinctive features of PWG.

A United Front

There were three major groups which formed the Naxalite operations. They were the Communist Party of India (Marxist – Leninist) [CPI (M-L)], the Peoples War Group (PWG) and the Maoist Communist Centre (MCC).[5] On 21September 2004, it was perceived that these three parties merged to form a new entity, the Communist Party of India-Maoist (CPI-Maoist). According to a CPI-Maoist press release issued by the 'General Secretary' of the Party, the merger was aimed at furthering the cause of "revolution" in India. The new party also pledged to work in close collaboration with the Communist Party of Nepal (Maoist). As part of its strategy, the CPI-Maoist would fiercely oppose the Central Government run by the Congress and its mainstream communist allies, the Communist Party of India (CPI) and the CPI-Marxist. The General Secretary also announced the formation of a 'People's Liberation Guerrilla Army' and extended support to "revolutionary struggles" in Nepal, Peru, the Philippines, Turkey and "other places".[6]

Causes for the Insurgency

Rural India has a long history of social hierarchy and discrimination through casteism and communalism, with the poor landless farmers being oppressed by high caste landlords. Whenever the landless peasants were driven against the wall and they reached their breaking point, India experienced sponsored uprisings like the Telangana and Naxalbari ones, with the Communists finding space to manoeuvre.

As per the census of 2001, there are 84.3 million tribal people (also known as Scheduled Tribes) in India. Tribal India inhabit the jungles and hilly areas, abundantly found in central India, which are also termed as Scheduled Areas (SA).[7] Several specific legislations have been enacted by the Central and State Governments, such as the Fifth Schedule (FS) and Panchayat (Extension to Scheduled Areas) Act (PESA) 1996, for the welfare and protection of tribal people and their tribal domain. These legislations have not been implemented in the desired manner.[8] Since times immemorial, the tribals have relied on the forests for their livelihood. In the 1980s, there were two developments which affected these people.

India's major source of power was from coal powered thermo-electric plants. The country was facing power shortage. In order to increase the generation capacity, the government resorted to opening new thermo power stations, simultaneously increasing the production of coal. Coal was found abundantly in central India. New coal mines were commissioned, leading to the displacement of a number of tribals from the states of Chattisgarh, Jharkhand, Madhya Pradesh and southern Uttar Pradesh. This large scale displacement of economically weak tribals which relied primarily on the forests for their livelihood is in all probability, the largest displacement of people, mandated by the government's development programmes.[9]

The second development was in the passing of the Forest (Conservation) Act 1980, which was legislated in order to provide a higher level of protection to the forests and to regulate diversion of forest lands for non-forestry purposes, which can be concluded to imply commercial projects. This Act gave sweeping powers to the forest officials to prevent encroachment by the forest dwellers into the forests, which was their domain on which they relied for their sustenance. These poor tribal forest dwellers, who till now were law abiding citizens of the country found themselves to be on the wrong side of the law. This Act did not permit habitations to exist inside the forests, even if they existed before the law was passed. On the other hand, there was large scale mining activity in these mineral rich areas which further displaced the tribals.

As per a Report by an Expert Committee to the Planning Commission, the majority of Scheduled tribes still live in conditions of serious deprivation and poverty. The tribal people have remained backward in all aspects of human development including education, health, nutrition, etc. Apart from socio-economic deprivation, there has been a steady erosion of traditional tribal rights and their command over resources.[10] As a result of these aspects of neglect, poverty and the lack of access to the traditional means of livelihood the people came to be disenchanted. The Maoist found a fertile ground to sow the seeds of their ideology and foment an insurgency.

Maoist Strategy and Tactics

In a press statement dated October 14, 2004, General Secretaries of the Central Committee of the two outfits, the MCC and the PWG, declared:

> *"The immediate aim and programme of the Maoist party is to carry on and complete the already on-going and advancing New Democratic Revolution in India as a part of the world proletarian revolution by overthrowing the semi-colonial, semi-feudal system under the neo-colonial form of indirect rule, exploitation and control... This revolution will be carried out and completed through armed agrarian revolutionary war, i.e. protracted people's war with the armed seizure of power remaining as its central and principal task, encircling the cities from the countryside and thereby finally capturing them. Hence the countryside as well as the Protracted People's War will remain as the "centre of gravity" of the party's work, while urban work will be complimentary to it."* [11]

The Document - Strategy & Tactics of the Indian Revolution'

The Maoists or namely the Naxalites, are also referred to as Left Wing Extremists. The CPI (Maoist) continue to be prevalent as the most dominant among the various Left Wing Extremist groups, accounting for more than 90% of total Left Wing Extremist incidents and 95% of resultant killings.[12] The Central Committee of the CPI (Maoist) have prepared and released a document titled 'Strategy & Tactics of the Indian Revolution' in September 2004. Five draft documents were prepared between February 2003 and September 2004 before the present text took shape. The document is divided into two parts comprising a total of thirteen chapters. Part I deals with 'Strategy' and comprises eight chapters. Part II deals with 'Tactics' discussed in five chapters. When this document is analysed there are a number of salient points which highlight the seriousness of the intent of the Maoists to overthrow the Government of India and establish their rule.

Analysis of the Document

Chapters one to five trace the history of revolutions which have occurred in the past and proceed to explain the situation in India as seen by the eyes of the CPI (Maoist). The third chapter analyses the various classes of Indian society such as the landlords, landless and peasants. Thereafter, the various stages of the Indian revolution being waged by the Maoists is explained.

Chapter six titled 'The Central Task of the Revolution – Seizure of political power by Armed force', amplifies Mao Tse Tung's teachings of seizing power by armed force. The text clearly and unambiguously elaborates that the aim of the revolution is to overthrow the Indian government by defeating the armed forces. It states, *"The Central task of the Indian revolution also is the seizure of political power. To accomplish this Central task, the Indian people will have to be organised in the people's army and will have to wipe out the armed forces of the counterrevolutionary Indian state through war and will have to establish, in its place, their own state."* Analysis of this chapter effectuates the following points regarding the conception and strategy of the Maoists:

- India is a very large country and the development and modernisation is not consistent in all areas, with some areas being more developed than others. This skewered development has caused resentment in the minds of the farmers. There have been uprisings by landless farmers in the past. The backwardness of certain areas and the grievances of the poor will be used as fuel to the fire for the insurgency.

- The Maoists will focus on land related issues to infuse their ideology on the tribals. They will take an example of the Naxal uprising in West Bengal and the land related problems of Andhra Pradesh. The peasants will be recruited into their army.

- The Maoists will initiate the insurgency in under developed areas. In these areas, poverty and other adverse social conditions are more widespread as compared to the conditions in the more developed states and cities. The backward areas and the people inhabiting these areas can thus be influenced with their ideology and will be more agreeable to participate in the insurgency.

- The Maoists will employ guerrilla tactics and employ this form of warfare to preserve themselves against a numerically superior force which is also armed better.

- The Maoists consider themselves to be at a more advantageous position in guerrilla warfare in the hinterland of the country in comparison to the security forces. They will accomplish to establish Base areas[13] and liberated zones as per the teachings of Mao.

- The Maoists will take advantage of political rivalry between various parties in states and manipulate it to be an ace up their sleeves as seen in WB etc. Aim will always be to further their interests

- The Maoists will focus on a protracted insurgency and will refrain from an all-out war, since they do not have to expedite the establishment of a new state.

- The Maoists consider the morale of the security forces low. As most of the security forces are locals (state police cadres) they have an affinity towards the insurgents as compared to the state.

- The Maoists accept that they are much weaker as compared to the security forces. They must always attack from a position of advantage to help preserve their forces.

- To overcome their disadvantage of force strength and quality, they aim to recruit a large number of insurgents which will enable to subdue the security forces.

- Many states of India are witnessing local insurgencies like J&K and Assam. The CPI (M) will try and forge a united front to fight the Indian Armed Forces, thus stretching the armed forces to an extreme.

- They are convinced that they will be able to defeat the Indian Armed Forces and Security forces eventually. They are also convinced that this will be done slowly – thus the protracted nature of war.

- Conditions favourable for creating favourable climate for their success is war with neighbouring countries, interstate politics caused by political parties and discontent within the armed and security forces.

- Their ultimate aim is to divide India on lines of class. They will support covertly uprisings for partitioning states like AP etc. and escalate land issues.

- The Maoists do not want to participate in the political process as a means to further their aim of overthrowing the government. They are of the opinion that by participating in elections and entering politics, it will divert the attention of the oppressed people from an armed struggle.

- They will not participate in elections which imply that they do not seek a political solution. They want to seize power through the barrel of the gun.

Chapter seven is titled Agrarian Revolution - People's Army -Base Areas. The important points are:-

- A revolutionary force comprising of armed farmers, peasants and the oppressed classes will form the backbone of the guerrilla army.

- Great stress and importance is laid on motivating the poor

farmers and landless, farm labourers and tribals to participate
in the insurgency. These people will be the soldiers and will
be recruited. The Maoist realise that without the support of
the people, the insurgency will not be successful. They will
start their recruitment in backward areas, where it is easier to
influence the people with their ideology.

- To achieve this, they will attract the labourers and landless
farmers with the promise of giving them power. Once the
insurgency has been able to consolidate itself, the power will
actually shift to the Central Committee.

- Once the army is formed, the Maoists will concentrate on
establishing base areas and thereafter consolidating their
position. These base areas will be used for training, equipping,
motivating the people and forming launch pads for operations.
They give great importance to motivating those recruited with
ideology and training them in the art of guerrilla warfare.
They will refine tactics based on the response of the security
forces. All tactics will be based on the local conditions and
need to be adaptable and flexible to the situation, keeping the
long term goal in mind.

- The insurgency will commence their armed struggle from
the most backward, economically weak, undeveloped and
neglected parts of India and geographically suitable for
guerrilla warfare such as jungles and mountainous areas.

- In such areas, the government rule will not be strong.
Therefore, the Maoists will concentrate their forces in these
areas and try and 'liberate' them from the government rule.

- They are prepared for a fluid battle, in which they will readily
give up areas where they have consolidated their position
earlier if the security forces are able to drive them out. Thus
base areas may change to guerrilla zones[14] and vice versa.

- They plan to consolidate their position in the areas of
Dandakaranya, Jharkhand, Andhra, Bihar, Orissa Border,
North Telangana, Koel-Kaimur. They will forge a contiguous
guerrilla zone in these belts, with each area influencing the

other. They aim to utilise their influence in these areas to spread the war to other parts, developing them into guerrilla zones, slowly spreading the war to the entire country.

- They are exploring the possibility of spreading the insurgency to the coastal regions and hitting maritime traffic, with an aim to disrupt supply routes.

- The insurgency will spread to the border areas. These border regions will get consolidated into base areas in the long term. This will facilitate external support, especially in the supply of arms and ammunition.

- The Maoist leadership realises that districts which are economically developed and have good road and transportation systems and are economically better off will be hard to win through force. Propaganda war will be carried out in these areas.

- They give great importance to areas which are near urban centres and are semi urban themselves. They aim to form clandestine groups. These groups will try and influence the people living in these areas with their ideology, exploiting those who are economically weaker - the working class. It is from here that they will spread further into urban areas.

- Their strategy consists of creating and consolidating the people's army and thereafter seizing political power in the areas where they are in control. We see this already happening in localities under the control of the Maoists. Such localities are governed not by the laws as laid down by the Indian Constitution but by 'Maoists laws'.[15]

- The insurgent army will be equipped with weapons looted and captured from the security forces. Attacks will be carried out by the cadres concentrating en-masse for the attack and thereafter quickly dispersing.

- The insurgency will be conducted in waves. They will use the phases of lull to consolidate their position by infusing their ideology on the insurgents, training and broadening their support base.

- The document stresses on studying and analysing the targeted areas for exploitation with their ideology in both economic and political issues. The document also stresses on the cadres carrying out a thorough study of the terrain and assessing the strengths and weaknesses of the security forces. Therefore, it can be concluded that when the Maoists carry out guerrilla attacks on the security forces, they are well prepared and know the terrain thoroughly.

- The document brings out the need to use NGOs and other sympathisers to their cause for expanding the insurgency.

- Having 'Liberated' an area, the Maoists are prepared to face oppressive action from the state machinery in terms of an economic blockade and any atrocities that may be committed.

- The CPI (Maoists) plan to first develop base areas in the backward and under developed regions of the country. Thereafter, the urban areas will also be targeted.

- The Maoists plan to first target the people who have migrated to the cities from the villages and are now working in the private industrial sector. This section of the population has their roots in rural areas and thus can identify with their insurgency.

- The Maoist leadership realises that they can obtain technological expertise, information and logistics supplies from the urban population sympathetic to the insurgency. Thus they lay great importance in recruiting this section of society. Hence the Government of India can expect the insurgency to spread to the cities.

- The final aim is to create Liberated Areas. Liberated Areas as the name suggests are those areas in which the Maoists have been able to gain complete control and their writ runs and not the government's.

Chapter eight brings out the importance of the Party, the People's Army and the United Front and goes on to analyse their importance in the light of the teachings of Mao. Part II deals with Tactics. Chapter nine is on building the 'Party' chapter ten, an important chapter is on the 'Peoples' Army'. Chapter eleven is on the 'United Front. The last two Chapters twelve and thirteen, talk about Special Social Sections & Nationalities and work in urban areas. Chapter ten, when analysed, brings out the following points:-

- The insurgent forces are well organised into:

    - **Main Force**. The Main Forces are the back bone of the PLGA and are equipped with the best arms and equipment possessed by the Maoists. They are trained and organised on the lines of a regular army. The main forces are composed of platoons and companies and special action teams. These forces will move to areas which need augmenting. They are under the control of the Commissions / Commands and operate anywhere on their instructions. These forces will be pitted against the security forces of the state, in co-ordination with the other two forces. In these encounters, the insurgents will endeavour to seize arms and ammunition from the security forces. They will try and encircle the security forces and be brutal in their action.

    - **Secondary Force**. The Secondary Forces are the local guerrilla squads organised at District level. They operate within their area of responsibility. Their weapons are inferior to those held by the Main Force. This force is good at fighting and employs guerrilla tactics.

    - **Base Force**. The Base Force is the self-defence squads or the Peoples' Militia. This force is the foundation for recruitment into the other two forces and PLGA. This force is where indoctrination and training commences. They are armed with assorted weapons.

- The Peoples Liberation Guerrilla Army is organised and divided into various branches like any other army. They have branches for Communication, Intelligence, Logistics, Ordinance, Artillery, Medical and Politico-military Training.

- The insurgency as per Mao's teachings is in the stage of Strategic Self Defence.[16] The insurgent forces are weaker than the security forces. The Maoists expect the state to react by sending in large forces to put down the insurgency. The Maoist ''People's Army' will carry out asymmetric warfare by exploiting the weaknesses of the security forces and pitting them against their strengths.

- In the second stage of war, as per the teachings of Mao, the state will consolidate its forces and encircle the Maoists strongholds. In executing their counter-offensive, the Maoists will not try and hold ground but will retreat, regroup and counter-attack from exterior lines.

- The Maoists will attack the security forces' communication nodes, out-posts and headquarters. These attacks will be carried out by night in the plains and by day and night in the jungle areas and hilly tracts. For these tactics to succeed, the Maoists place great importance on the support and indoctrination of the local population and knowledge of the terrain.

- The Maoists plan to keep on opening new fronts so as to give themselves room to manoeuvre when the security forces intensify their action.

- The Maoists know that guerrilla warfare will not be able to ensure them victory. But they are aware of the advantages of this kind of warfare when pitted against a stronger force. They aim to lower the morale of the security forces by keeping them under prolonged pressure and striking when least expected. Small victories will lead to larger ones and they will slowly consolidate, moving on to mobile warfare.

- Mobile warfare is also discussed in detail and the Maoists will resort to this level of warfare after consolidation and expansion of their army. They will choose the place for attack and time to retreat.

- As per the document, when the Maoists are able to launch a counter-offensive on the security forces, they will resort to positional warfare, aiming to win and hold ground. This will be the last phase of their war.

When read and understood in its entirety, this document gives the Maoists a blue-print for waging the insurgency. When analysed with the insurgency as seen on the ground, we can see that they are more or less playing by their book. The patterns of attacks by the Maoists are in keeping with the document. Though they are still in the first stage of strategic defensive, they are working to move onto the second stage by consolidating their position. Once they are able to get external support in the form of arms and ammunition, the Maoist will be well equipped to move onto the next phase. The insurgency is spreading across India as per plan. Urban areas are being targeted and so are the Border States in a bid to link up with external agencies for support.

Areas Affected by the Insurgency

On the 06 July 2010, the Home Secretary, Mr GK Pillai made a statement that 220 districts in India had experienced incidents of LWE. Of these, 34 Districts have been classified as worst affected and 83 districts are slightly or partially affected by the problem. [17](The MHA Annual Report of 2010-2011 quotes 35 districts.) As of 31 October 2011, there were 182 Districts affected by LWE.[18] The Maoist insurgency is wide spread over India with 20 of the 28 states of India being affected.[19] The states of Andhra Pradesh, Bihar, Chattisgarh, Jharkhand, Madhya Pradesh, Maharashtra, Orissa, Uttar Pradesh and West Bengal experienced the maximum violence.[20] The Maoists have also spread their tentacles to the eastern states of Assam, Tripura and Arunachal Pradesh. They have linked up with the ULFA as confirmed by Prakash Baruah.[21] In the west, the border states of Punjab and Rajasthan have also witnessed incidents of LWE. Southern India has not been spared, and the states of Karnataka, Tamil Nadu and Kerala have experienced incidents of LWE. In a bid to target urban areas, the CPI (Maoist) have formed a 'Golden Corridor Committee' to build its base in the industrial areas of Gujarat and Maharashtra, stretching from Pune to Ahmedabad, including commercial hubs like Mumbai, Nashik, Surat and Vadodara.[22]

As per a study carried out by the Centre of Land Warfare, of the

35 worst affected districts[23], there are four areas or 'fault lines' which are severely affected. They are[24]:-

- The Orissa Andhra Fault Line.

- The Southern Chattisgarh Fault Line. This includes Gadchiroli district of Maharashtra and Balaghat district of Madhya Pradesh.

- The Jharkhand Fault line. This includes West Midnapore district of West Bengal.

- South Bihar Fault line.

The Peoples Liberation Guerrilla Army (PLGA)

The Central Military Commission (CMC) heads the Maoist military arm. Though there are different military and political structures, there are many members common to both. An organisation chart is placed as an appendix. At present, the Maoists have a PLGA, which they aim to transform into the People's Liberation Army.[25] As covered in the analysis of the document titled 'Strategy & Tactics of the Indian Revolution', the PLGA is organised in the form of a regular army with three kinds of Forces.

Strength. This army has an estimated strength of 8,000 to 12,000 cadres.[26] Majority of its cadres are young, being in the age group of 14 to 25 years.[27] Women cadres have also been recruited into the PLGA. An estimate of the force levels in various regions is appended.

Table - Estimated Armed Force Level[28]

SC/SAC/SOC/SCZ	Military Battalion	Military Company	Platoons	Militia Platoons
DKSCZ (Dandakaranya Special Zone Committee)		10	23	40
AOBSCZ (Assam Odisha Bengal Special Zone Committee)		1	3	1
MRSC (Maharashtra Rayalaseema Special Committee)		0	2	0
WBSC (West Bengal Speacial Committee)		0	3	3
BJNCSAC (Bihar Jharkhand North Chhattisgarh Special Area Committee)		3-4	8	30
NTSCZ (North Telangana Special Zone Committee)		0	1	0
CRC* (Central Region Committee)	1	1	0	0
ERC** (Eastern Region Committee)	1 (Under Progress)	1	0	0
TOTAL	**2**	**18-19**	**40**	**74**

*   Reflects ability to operate in battalion strength.

**   Ability to operate in battalion strength under progress.

Arms. The Maoists are estimated to have a weapon holding of 15,000 to 20,000 assorted weapons which include 900 X AK-47/AK-56 rifles, 200 X light machine guns (LMGs) and 100 X 2" mortars / grenade firing rifles.[29] They also have an assortment of INSAS rifles, .303 rifles, double and single barrel guns and locally manufactured guns. Reports also indicate that the Maoist cadres are also equipped with AK-47 assault rifles, supplied by the LTTE and ISI.[30] They also loot weapons from the police[31] and possess IEDs which have been fabricated by them using locally available material such as urea, diesel, potassium and ammonium nitrate. They have even innovated trigger devices from bamboo.[32]

Training. The PLGA is known for its cohesiveness and well trained manpower. It has a Central Military Instructors Team (CMIT) to impart training to their cadres. This team is under the Central Military Commission (CMC).[33] There are indications that retired army or other security forces personnel who train the cadres in field craft and weapon training.[34]

Training is given great stress and importance by the PLGA. The training camps are located in thick jungles, which are inhospitable with thick forest cover and deep ravines. Such terrain gives the Maoists the ideal training ground to train for guerrilla warfare. At the same time, they are at a convenient distance from habitation so as to provide for logistics support. Training is carried out in manageable groups of around 20 to 22 trainees, and the trainees are not limited to one state of origin, but collective training is conducted for cadres from different states.[35]

The PLGA's basic military course teaches weapon training, map reading and basic field and battle craft. Instead of commencing training with actual weapons, the trainees first learn how to handle wooden replicas or dummy weapons and slowly they graduate to actual weapons. A limited amount of live firing is carried out by the novices due to the paucity of ammunition. The trainees who perform well in live firing are given further training on more modern weapons.[36] Manuals recovered from training camps indicate that the PLGA is modelled on the lines of a regular army. These manuals are written in languages spoken by the trainees, like Telugu. The training manuals even analyse past operations, indicating that they refine their training as per the lessons learnt from these operations. The manuals are extensive in content and include a vast number of topics on military field training.[37] Apart from the basic training, the training syllabus stresses on practical aspects of collection of intelligence, map reading, living off the land and study of the tactics followed by the security forces, ambush and raid with special emphasis to looting of arms.[38] Advanced training on coded communication, field signals, retreat, regroup and rendezvous and appreciation of the battle situation is also imparted. Selected cadres are given specialised training for assembling IEDs.[39] The Maoists have been successful in training their cadres well, which can be seen from the manner in which they conduct operations against the security forces and how successful they are in these operations.

Anticipating the use of airpower against the insurgency, the insurgents have also trained their cadres in aspects of air defence. They have mastered facets of passive air defence and are also training for active air defence. A training manual titled 'Guerrilla Air Defence: Anti-Aircraft Weapons and Techniques for Guerrilla Forces', published by Palladin Press, Colorado, USA has been recovered from them.[40] The Maoists' air defence syllabus includes passive air defence topics on camouflage and concealment, dispersal techniques, targeting aircraft with LMGs, small weapons, etc. It also describes how helicopters and aircrafts work. They have been trained for firing against a moving airborne target, evident from the attacks on Indian Air Force Helicopters.[41] A document seized by the police quotes:

> *"We have to increase recruitment into PLGA on a large scale. We have to give training to PLGA, militia and others on a wide scale by preparing a higher-level training syllabus to face air attacks of the Indian Air Force."* [42]

Intelligence Network. The Naxals have put in place a formidable intelligence network not just in Chhattisgarh but even in adjoining states of Jharkhand, Orissa, Bihar and Andhra Pradesh. Keeping in line with a military set up, the PLGA has two intelligence agencies, the Military Intelligence and the 'Peoples Secret Service (PSS)'.[43]

The Military Intelligence gathers intelligence about security forces. Before every attack on security personnel the Military Intelligence of the Naxals prepares an elaborate blueprint with all relevant details, complete with a map, which is given to the cadres to carry out the strike. The PSS is used primarily for the purpose of gathering information about district and local administration, about the various development projects being carried out and for planning kidnappings.

To facilitate intelligence gathering, the Maoists have a very wide spread network of informers who are sympathetic to their cause and support the Maoists. These informers monitor the activities of the security personnel and other civil administrative officials and pass the information on to the intelligence agencies in real time.[44]

Planning Operations. All operations conducted by the Maoists against the security forces or civil administrative machinery, are well planned. They carry out a complete and detailed study of the terrain and other intelligence inputs received from their wide-spread network of informers. This facilitates in planning for all types of contingencies before they launch the operation. The insurgents also take advantage of the lack of inter-state coordination between the police forces, particularly at the police stations at state borders.[45] Whenever the Maoists carry out raids, they do so after meticulous planning, reconnaissance and rehearsals. The raid on the NALCO at Panchapatli mines, Damanjodi in the Koraput district of Orissa was planned over a period of six months.[46]

Analysis of a Maoist propaganda document claims the attack on a Greyhound Force on 29 June 2008 was well planned and efficiently executed. Of the 65 personnel on board a boat, only 29 swam to safety after the attack.[47] The article in a CPI (Maoist) Information Bulletin 20 July 2008 states:[48]

"The June 29 attack by the Maoist guerrillas was meticulously planned and daringly executed in accordance with the Maoist principles of guerrilla war. Following the Maoist dictum to lure the enemy deep into the guerrilla territory and hit him where it is advantageous to the guerrillas, a bait was first placed by spreading the rumour that a conclave of top Maoist leaders was being held in Orissa's Malkangiri district. Like dogs lured by the scent of meat the Greyhounds walked into this trap and thought they would get a big prize. After around four days of hectic combing when they found no trace of the supposed meeting they retraced their way back to Andhra Pradesh. They had two options: either take the much longer forest route or the faster river route to reach the local operational HQs in Chitrakonda and from there to Andhra Pradesh. Being unaccustomed to the local terrain and fearing probable ambush by the Maoists, they

thought it safer to take the river route. Moreover, however much these state-hired mercenaries were trained in jungle warfare they were reluctant to take the longer land route for it is quite tiresome. And the Maoist guerrillas, who had been keenly following the movements of the Greyhounds based on timely intelligence inputs by the local people and their scouts, lay in waiting to take on the enemy forces whether they go back through the forest route or river route. Luckily for the Maoists, the enemy forces decided to travel back in a single launch which made it easier for the guerrillas to inflict the maximum damage and greater casualties to the enemy. Thus they met their watery grave.[49]

Protection of Base Areas. To protect their base areas and liberated areas, the Maoists have organised a three/four tier defence. For example, in the area of Abujhmadh, the insurgents are organised in four tiers. The outer tier is patrolled by the 'jan militia' which has assorted weapons. The local militia squads are static, while the other tiers are mobile. A large number of mines and IEDs are also laid out. The second / third tier is held by the special militia / local squads who also possess an array of weapons and some small arms. The fourth tier (inner most) is well defended being held by the well trained local guerrilla squads with the core being defended by the well trained and equipped main force.[50]

Tactics. The Maoists tactics consist of assaults/attacks, ambushes, kidnappings and assassinations, use of IEDs and the destruction of government infrastructure.[51] The Maoists do not utilise the local population during these raids. The reason is that the Maoists are aware that the local population is the centre of gravity in the insurgency. If they are used during attacks, the insurgents may lose their support.[52]

Assaults/Attacks. Assaults/attacks are mainly carried out to loot arms from the security forces, so as to equip their cadres and are executed by the Maoists mainly in large numbers. Such assaults have also been termed as 'swarming attacks'. This tactic has been adopted from the Nepali Maoists.[53] When these attacks are analysed, data indicates that normally a force of 200 to 300 Maoists carry out attacks on targets like police stations, villages or construction sites. In 2004, a thousand strong Maoist force attacked the District Headquarter at

Koraput, Odisha. Approximately 200 weapons were looted. There are innumerable incidents wherein the insurgents have attacked armouries to loot weapons and ammunition.[54] These assaults are carried out after careful planning, rehearsals and co-ordination, which adheres to the principles enumerated in the CPI (Maoist) document, 'Strategy & Tactics of the Indian Revolution' and the document 'Functioning of Military Commissions and Commands - Coordination of Main, Secondary and Base Forces.'[55] Planning is carried out at the highest level of CMC/CRC[56] and the raid is executed only after there is a high probability of success, as analysed from the success of their attacks.

Ambush. Ambushes are executed by the insurgents in a bid to blunt the offensive campaign of the security forces.[57] These ambushes which are quite successful would have an adverse effect on the security forces when on patrol by keeping them under constant battle pressure, resulting in fatigue, which in turn would affect their morale. The insurgents have evolved their own tactics of mobile and one point ambushes.[58] The amount of planning that goes into ambushes is evident from the ambush on a CRPF patrol on 03 May 2011 in Lohardaga District in Jharkhand. As per reports, eleven security CRPF personnel were killed and forty were injured in the ambush. The insurgents had planted IEDs at intervals of one to two feet.[59] The Maoist's version is recounted in an article from one of the 'Monthly Information Bulletins," a publication released by the Maoists. It states regarding an attack on the CRPF:

"On May 3, a daring and dashing ambush was conducted by the PLGA near Urumuri village near the Dhardharia falls in Lohardagga district. More than a company force consisting of CRPF and Jharkhand armed joint forces were returning from Urumuri when they got caught in the ambush. A circle of mines was planted within 500 metres of radius at a distance of ten feet. The PLGA allowed the enemy forces to enter this circle and conducted a surprise attack. Fourteen policemen died and about sixty to sixty five of them were injured."[60]

Kidnappings. Kidnappings of high value individuals such as District Collectors and politicians are carried out to extract concession from the government. Kidnappings of low value individuals are also carried out to instil fear in the local population and force them to obey the verdicts of 'janta sarkars',[61] or for ransom.

India has no formal policy to deal with kidnappings. In most cases, demands of the kidnappers are agreed to, especially where there is high visibility of the incident in the media. These demands are usually for the release of individuals arrested by the police on suspicion of being involved in the insurgency. By being able to make the government to agree to its demands, the insurgents are able to project themselves the protectors of the population. Such a policy encourages kidnappings and the Maoists will continue to resort to this tactic, till a strong no bargaining policy, as followed by countries such as the USA and Israel, is formulated.

Assassinations and Killings. The Maoists carry out assassinations and killings in their bid to instil fear in the local population and gain their obedience and support. They also kill to create a power and governance vacuum in rural areas and the space is filled by them.[62] Suspected 'police informers' are regularly killed. Villagers who do not obey the Maoists or believe in their ideology are also targeted. In order to demonstrate their ability in undermining the state, the insurgents have also attempted to target important individuals like the CMs of Andhra Pradesh and West Bengal. Killings are also carried out to help in extorting money. The net effect of these killings is reducing the faith of the common man on the police force and instilling fear and respect in the eyes of the people.[63]

Use of Improvised Explosive Devices (IEDs). The insurgents regularly mine roads to deny the security forces the use of roads and restrict their mobility. As per the Additional Director General (Operations) of the CRPF:-

"Landmines and IEDs are most serious problems faced by CRPF and other forces deployed in Maoist-hit states. Almost 70 per cent of the casualties of the Forces are due to triggering of IEDs by Naxals."[64]

The Maoists owe their success in utilisation of IEDs by the availability of large quantities of explosives looted by them and availability of cadres who were involved in mining activities and are conversant with working with explosives.[65] They are innovative in fabricating triggering devices with bamboo and even hypodermic syringes. Innocuous pieces of red ribbons mark mined areas and patrolling cadres are always on the lookout for these indications.

Destruction of Government Infrastructure.   In a bid to countermine the authority of the state and show governance structures at field levels as being ineffective, the Maoists prevent the execution and implementation of development works including infrastructure like railways, roads, power and telecom.[66] As per their propaganda to the people, any development work carried out by the government is a sign of oppression and therefore should be prohibited.[67] By blowing up roads and bridges, the Maoists impose barriers on the local population and deny the accessibility of the people to the outside world.[68] They also consider roads a threat to their survival.

State Response and Problem Areas

The Government of India is treating the Maoist insurgency as a pure law and order problem. It has given the primary responsibility of handling this insurgency to the naxal affected states in a co-ordinated manner.[69] The government has also drawn up a policy which was given in a status paper prepared by the Ministry of Home Affairs and brought out in May 2008. The salient points of this policy are[70]:

- Deal sternly with the Naxalites indulging in violence.

- Address the problem simultaneously on political, security and development fronts in a holistic manner.

- Ensure inter-state coordination in dealing with the problem.

- Accord priority to faster socio-economic development in the Naxal affected or prone areas.

- Supplement the efforts and resources of the affected states on both security and development fronts.

- Promote local resistance groups against the Naxalites.

- Use mass media to highlight the futility of Naxal violence and the loss of life and property caused by it.

- Have a proper surrender and rehabilitation policy for the Naxalites.

- Affected states will not have any peace dialogue with the Naxal groups, unless the latter agree to give up violence and arms.

One of the reasons for the spread of Left Wing Extremism is the lack of local governance in the affected areas and associated problems of dearth of development, security etc.[71] On examining the response policy, it can be concluded that the government aims to adopt a two pronged strategy of security and development. The Government of India created a new division called the 'Naxal Management Division' under the Ministry of Home Affairs on 19 October 2006. This Division is mandated with effectively tackling the Naxal insurgency from both security and development angles.[72] The Naxal Management Division has adopted a strategy to deal with the Maoist problem by addressing areas of security, development, ensuring rights of local communities, improvement in governance and public perception management.[73] A great amount of attention has been given to development of Naxal affected areas and good governance and various schemes have been initiated.[74]

Security. The security related strategy is purely manpower intensive. It is aimed at increasing the strength of police and paramilitary forces in the insurgency affected areas. In 2003, a Group of Ministers assigned the Central Reserve Police Force (CRPF) the responsibility for counter-insurgency operations, in support of police across the country.[75] The government has also been augmenting the State police forces with various para-military forces. 74 battalions of Central Armed Police Forces (CAPFs) and Commando Battalions for Resolute Action (CoBRA) teams are currently deployed for assisting the State Police in the States of Andhra Pradesh, Bihar, Chhattisgarh, Jharkhand, Madhya Pradesh, Maharashtra, Odisha, Uttar Pradesh and West Bengal. 37 India Reserve (IR) battalions were sanctioned to nine naxal affected States, of which 34 have been raised. The government has approved the raising of ten new Specialised India Reserve Battalions (SIRBs) in the LWE States of Bihar, Chhattisgarh, Jharkhand, Madhya Pradesh, Odisha and West Bengal, which are to be raised during 2011-12 to 2013-14. Ten Battalions of Specialised Force trained and equipped for counterinsurgency and jungle-warfare operations, named as Commando Battalions for Resolute Action

(CoBRA) have been raised as a part of the Central Reserve Police Force (CRPF) during the period from 2008-09 to 2010-11 and have been deployed in the LWE affected States.[76] Under the Modernisation of State Police Forces Scheme (MPF Scheme), the States' police forces and their intelligence apparatus are being modernised and upgraded. The government is also providing assistance in training the police forces with the assistance of the Ministry of Defence, the Central Police Organisations and the Bureau of Police Research and Development [77]

Despite these large numbers of security forces which have been pumped in to beef up the security environment in the insurgency affected States, the rule of the Maoists still prevails. Wherever the police and paramilitary forces have been successful in subduing the insurgents, it has just resulted in the insurgents to shift their base to a neighbouring area.

Development. Towards developing the insurgency affected areas, the central government has provided funds to the States towards various Central Schemes such as:[78]

- Backward Regions Grant Fund.

- Mahatma Gandhi National Rural Employment Guarantee Scheme.

- Prime Minister's Gram Sadak Yojana, National Rural Health Mission.

- Ashram Schools.

- Rajiv Gandhi Grameen Vidhyutikaran Yojana.

- Sarva Siksha Abhiyan.

- The Ministry of Road Transport & Highways has been implementing Road Requirement Plan. Under this plan, major roads required for connectivity are being built in LWE areas.

- Aiming to provide public infrastructure and services in LWE affected areas; the Planning Commission is implementing the Integrated Action Plan (IAP) in 78 selected Districts for accelerated development.

- Forest land will be utilised to build infrastructure such as schools, dispensaries/hospitals, electrical and telecommunication lines, drinking water, water/rain water harvesting structures, minor irrigation canal, non-conventional sources of energy, vocational training centres, power sub-stations, rural roads, communication posts; and police establishments like police stations/outposts/border outposts/ watch towers in sensitive areas and laying of optical fibre cables, telephone lines & drinking water supply lines.

Problem Areas

Lack of Secure Environment. To ensure the success of these schemes and development in the affected areas, a pre-requisite would be to have a secure and peaceful environment conducive for such development work. The Maoists are making all efforts to sabotage this development and prevent the construction of roads, power and telecom projects by violence and terror tactics, aiming to portray the ineffectiveness of the local governance.[79] The success of the government's development projects would help towards removing the grievances of poor development in LWE areas and win the hearts and minds of the local population, who are the centre of gravity in the fight against the insurgency. For example, Chhattisgarh, the State with the worst history of Naxal violence over the last decade, is finding it difficult to implement the Centre's ambitious road construction projects in areas affected by left wing extremism. Of the 44 road projects sanctioned in the State under the first phase of the Centre's plan, only three were completed by the end of 2011. The first plan was approved in February 2009.[80] Schools are without teachers and hospitals without doctors. These professionals do not want to be posted to such insecure areas and there is political interference in respect of such postings.[81] The State Government also opines that these projects can only be undertaken if a secure environment exists and the writ of law prevails.[82] Statistics indicate that a larger number of Security personnel have been killed by the Maoists as compared to the number of Maoists killed by the Security personnel.[83]It is evident that the Maoists are still in control of most of the insurgency affected zones. The Security Forces have been unable to provide a safe environment for development of these areas, setting back the very strategy adopted by the government.

Untrained Police Force. The State police forces are established and organised to maintain law and order of the State. They are accordingly trained for maintaining law and order and other related activities. Therefore, they are not trained for combatting insurgency, which requires a specialised force to do so. The CRPF which has been mandated to combat the insurgency is not a specialised counterinsurgency force.[84]

As per the recommendations of the UN, a peacetime police-to population ratio of 222 policemen per 100,000 citizens should be maintained. India falls drastically short of this ratio.[85] In 2010, the ratio in Orissa was 135.8, West Bengal - 100 and Bihar was just 74.29. The ratios have improved in Jharkhand to 206.98 and Chattisgarh has the best ratio of 226.3.[86]

In a bid to make good the shortfall of police personnel, the government has expedited the process of recruitment. 36 Battalions comprising over 36,000 personnel have been raised after November 2008 and 21 more Battalions are being raised. The CAPFs recruited 91,761 constables in 2009-10 and 2010-11. State police forces have reported that they have recruited 1, 07,238 constables in 2009 and 90,359 in 2010. In 2011-12, CAPFs will recruit 92,168 constables and 29,370 officers and other ranks.[87] The quality of training imparted to such large numbers would definitely be a difficult task. Making up numbers is not the same as having a trained and experienced police force.

A major problem area in counterinsurgency operations is the large gestation period required for creating and training security forces to undertake counterinsurgency operations.[88] Training the police force to undertake anti naxal operations is estimated to take at least eight to ten years.[89] To fight the Maoist insurgency, the strength of the police force is being increased at a rapid pace. In Chattisgarh, the strength of the police force doubled to 50,000 in three years. However, has the number of training establishments or capacity of existing ones been increased? Are the levels of training of the police personnel to fight the insurgents who employ guerrilla tactics sufficient?

The CRPF has only six training centres to train their recruits. These centres can only train 150 to 200 recruits in a basic course which takes nine months. The number of CRPF personnel has increased from 1, 67,367 in 1999, to 2, 80,000 in 2010. New battalions are as per media reports being trained at improvised facilities lacking in basic infrastructure like classrooms, quality firing ranges and combat-simulation facilities.[90] The CRPF which has grown to 210 battalions by 2010 is not considered to be a specialised counterinsurgency force.[91]

Though the Maoist insurgency has been festering for a considerable period of time, clearance to set up a counterinsurgency warfare training institution, the 'National School of Counter Insurgency Warfare (NSCIW)' at Kondaigaon Chattisgarh has been given only in 2011. Once functional, this school will train police personnel for counterinsurgency operations.[92] In the State of Chattisgarh, where the levels of Naxal violence are high, Superintendents of Police (SPs) are given just 45 days of training at the Jungle School at Kanker. There is no fixed training period for the over 3,500 plus Special Police Officers (SOPs) employed in counterinsurgency operations. Their training can vary from one to three months.[93]

Six training schools will come up in different parts of the country to bring in professionalism in the men on the ground. These include CRPF intelligence institute in Gurgaon (Haryana), RAF training school in Meerut (UP) and Indian institute of IED management in Pune (Maharashtra).[94]However, it will take time before these schools are ready to impart training.

The Government has approved 21 Counter Insurgency and Anti-Terrorism Schools (CIATs) in the Eleventh Five Year Plan Period in Assam, Bihar, Chhattisgarh, Jharkhand, Orissa, West Bengal, Nagaland, Manipur and Tripura. Presently, 17 CIAT Schools are functional in the various States where several training courses are running for police personnel. About 18,389 police personnel have been trained till April, 2012 in these schools.[95]

As per an appraisal carried out by the Border Security Forces on police training, it would take eight to ten years to impart the required training to the police force, Central Police Organisation (CPO) and

CRPF in basic tactical skills. As per the opinion of an official of the Ministry of Home Affairs, Government of India, the training levels of the police force were 'abysmal'. The CRPF fired only 20 rounds a year towards training. In comparison, the training levels of the Maoists are much better. They (Maoists) had organised at least 93 training camps for their cadres in 2010.[96] The former DGP of Jharkhand, Mr Neyaz Ahmed, in an interview to a News channel was also of the opinion that training of police personnel was required and various drills had to be streamlined.[97] In another incident in August 2011, a team of 30 Naxals held off 250 police commandos for over 10 hours in Makadchuha village in Maharashtra's Gadchiroli district. The police force included commandos of the CRPF's CoBRA battalion, who have been specifically trained for anti-Naxal operations.[98] Inadequate combat capability, which is also a result of insufficient training of police forces in Naxal affected States is considered a primary reason for the inability of the police to control the Naxal insurgency.[99]

Trained CoBRA battalions have been deployed for election duties in the past. One such example is the State elections in Assam in 2011. There are reports which indicate that not all the CRPF personnel undergoing training at the Jungle Warfare School in Chhattisgarh's Kanker district are being used for counter-Maoist operations, but are being utilised for other duties such as the protection of VIPs. This further reduces the availability of trained manpower.

In Andhra Pradesh, the State was able to tackle the naxal insurgency with quite a bit of success. They raised the elite 'Greyhound' force to do so. This elite commando force, was raised in 1989.[100] Its main mandate is to deal with Left Wing Extremism which was rampant in the State. This force draws inspiration from the famous Selous Scouts (of Rhodesia) by borrowing their motto "The Bush War has to be fought in the Bushes".[101] It was only after a considerable amount of time that the Greyhound Force was able to bring the insurgency under control. The data in Table 1 indicates the number of Naxal related incidents reducing drastically from 2006 onwards.

DEATHS / INCIDENTS : ANDHRA PRADESH

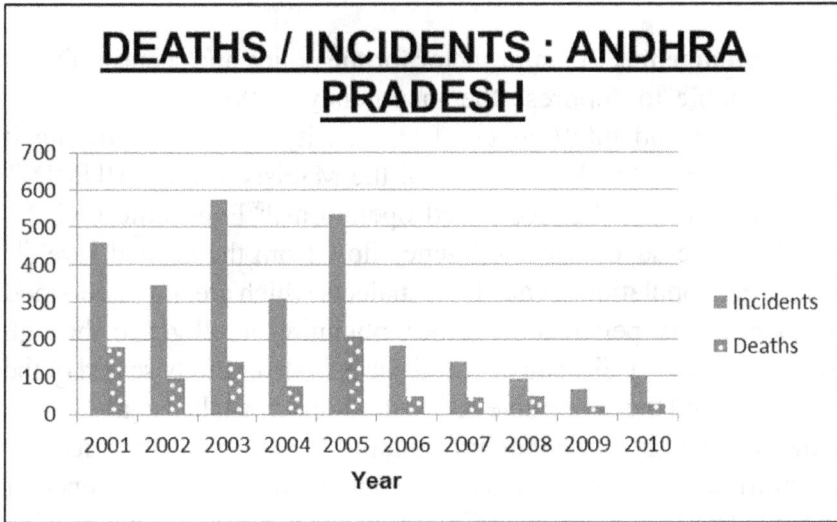

Table 1[102]

With the positive results achieved, the strength of this force was doubled to 2000 personnel in 2008.[103] This 2,000-strong Greyhound force is a well-trained, physically and mentally fit force, being imparted with special training in field craft and handling weapons.[104] To ensure high morale, they are better paid and equipped than State police cadres. The Greyhound forces are kept in good training by regularly undergoing refresher training.[105] High levels of training have definitely played a very important part in the ability of this force in controlling the insurgency.

The urgent requirement to address the criticality of quality training is summed up in an Occasional Paper by the IDSA - *"The police training system, infrastructure, resources, manpower and logistics support are far below the desired level. Training institutes fail to attract good trainers and cannot generate interest among trainees. Making up for the deficiency of training resources, is also a secondary priority, as the limited police budget is mostly exhausted among other heads, and training per se gets neglected. Most importantly, a positive environment and culture for training is generally lacking in the police. There is little commitment for training. Imparting or undergoing training is generally disliked and thrust upon. Posting to training institutions is considered as a punishment and generally avoided.*"[106]

Poor Intelligence. A major factor for the police and security forces being unable to suppress the insurgency is the lack of reliable information and intelligence. The security forces are finding it difficult to monitor the activities of the Maoists through HUMINT and carry out intelligence based operations.[107]Even elite CoBRA battalions are devoid of intelligence flow from the ground level.[108] The target population speaks local dialects which are not understood by the security personnel. Further, obtaining intelligence through informers is a very difficult task as the tribals are mortally scared of the insurgents and the oppressive action that would be taken against them if they are caught passing on information. A person usually becomes an informer due to reasons such as money, ideology, conscience or enmity. The locals are not affected by these reasons, thus making the task of recruiting informers a difficult one.[109]There is no lack of money that can be offered to informers. Though money would be a tempting offer, the fear of violent reprisals to the informers and their families is a better deterrent.[110] According to the Home Minister, out of 424 civilians killed in 2010 so far, 192 were informers.[111] There is a requirement to protect the informers so as to ensure that this avenue for obtaining intelligence does not get blocked.

The CRPF has only eight intelligence operatives per battalion, a very insignificant figure considering the task requirement.[112] The lack of intelligence is evident from what the Home Minister of India had to say while inaugurating the first-ever intelligence training school for Central Reserve Police Force (CRPF) officers and personnel, "*The CRPF, a key force in anti-Naxal operations, will have to acquire an intelligence - based strategy to combat Maoists who have organised themselves as a "regular fighting army.*"[113] This school will have the capacity to train only 500 personnel per year. These trained personnel will in turn train others in the battalions. Therefore, it will take time for the intelligence apparatus to start paying dividends.

The lack of intelligence also manifests itself in the problem of '*Lazy Generalship*'.[114] Devoid of intelligence, the counterinsurgent is tactically blind. This results in the induction of a large number of security personnel in the insurgency affected areas with the hope that due to their large numbers, they will have numerous chance encounters. These 'chance encounters' are usually to the disadvantage of the security forces as seen in Dantewada.

Poor Morale of Security Forces. Wrong policy decisions based on political compulsions at times create conditions responsible for lowering the morale of security forces. The decision taken by the Maharashtra Home Ministry to reduce the tempo of anti-Naxal operations so as to prevent casualties of security personnel is one such example. This decision was taken to prevent criticism by the opposition on the number of security personnel killed and injured in counterinsurgency operations. This dithering approach resulted in the security personnel not venturing out on long patrols and emboldened the Naxals in their attacks.[115] Political compulsions would surely lower the morale of the Security forces fighting with their hands tied behind their backs. This also leads to the troops not adhering to standard operating procedures which are responsible for numerous deaths of security personnel.[116] Some reasons for poor morale amongst the security forces are:

- **Poor Leadership.** Issues of poor leadership have plagued the CRPF.[117] As quoted by a police officer in one of the papers regarding anti naxal operations in Chattisgarh, "*Lack of vision in police leadership is severely hampering the anti-Naxal operations.*"[118] Mr ER Rammohan has also been critical of the leadership in the paramilitary forces engaged in anti-naxal operations.[119]

- **Long Tenures.** At times, the security personnel serve for long tenures under constant threat of attacks from the naxals. There are troops of the 1 Indian Reserve Battalion (IRB) in West Bengal that have served for eight years continuously carrying out anti- naxal operations.[120]

- **Poor Living Conditions.** CRPF troops have refused to occupy camps due to inhuman living conditions. The troops of 1 IRB even revolted to protest about their poor living conditions.[121]

- **Constant Pressure.** Due to being constantly under stress, a result of long tenures and nature of job, some troops commit suicide or even suffer from mental disorders.[122] 256 BSF troops have committed suicide from 2004 to 2011 as per data provided to the Rajya Sabha by the BSF and the Bureau of Police Research and Development. Reasons for suicide included high levels of stress.[123] A study conducted by the Indian Institute of Management at Ahmedabad also highlights that stress caused due to long working hours, continuous tenures in difficult areas and lack of health care facilities is responsible for numerous security forces personnel committing suicide.[124]

- **State of Equipment.** Despite a large amount of money being spent on modernisation, at times the state of equipment of the security forces is not up to the desired standards. Communication failure between a patrol and headquarters did not permit the troops to call for reinforcements when ambushed in the jungles of Chhattisgarh's Bijapur district in August 2011. This resulted in the deaths of ten security force personnel.[125]

Analysis of the Maoists

- The Maoists, have been able to influence the local population with their ideology and at present, do have support of the local population, which are the centre of gravity in the fight against the insurgency. They have been able to increase their geographical spread. There is a trend in the increase of the number of naxal related incidents and deaths due to naxal violence.

- They have a well organised political structure with an ideology which has an appeal to the poor landless and socially oppressed classes. They also have in place a well-defined military organisation on the lines of a regular army.

- Their cadres are sufficiently armed with a collection of arms – from kitchen and farming implements to modern weapons such as AK 47 rifles and rocket launchers. The PLGA has a Research and Development arm and Technical arm involved in the production of weapons.

- The PLGA is well trained in the art of war and are also motivated. They maintain strict discipline amongst the cadres.

- The insurgents have a well-developed intelligence network. All operations are meticulously planned and rehearsed based on intelligence gathered by their cadres.

- Naxalites have advantages in their area of operation. They have an in-depth knowledge of the terrain in which they operate. This terrain suites guerrilla warfare. Therefore, they enjoy tactical advantage.

- The Maoists are ruthless in their operations against the security forces. These tactics employed by the Maoists, instils a sense of fear in the police and other security forces. Regular victories in well planned operations, increases their morale.

- The Maoists operate from a position of advantage as they have the initiative in their operations.

- This insurgency is not a law and order problem but has a more serious connotation.

Analysis of State Response

- The Government of India is treating this movement as a law and order problem caused by poor governance. Therefore, it employs a police force to tackle the movement and has initiated development work in backward areas.

- There are areas which are not under the control of the State. There are other areas where the security forces are unable to provide a safe environment. Due to this, the government is unable to carry out development work in the highly affected areas.

- The security forces are well organised and armed. However, they are not trained for jungle and guerrilla warfare or counterinsurgency operations. It will take at least eight to ten years to be able to have a sufficiently trained police force in counterinsurgency operations.

- Due to a lack of ground level and actionable intelligence, the security forces are unable to plan any operations against the Maoists in a bid to take the initiative. This lack of intelligence results in aimless patrolling, which results in further casualties. The tactics employed by the security forces are therefore reactionary in nature.

- The security forces operate under great stress levels, poor leadership and at times very difficult living conditions. This has an adverse effect on their morale.

Strategy to Combat the Insurgency

In keeping with the lines of the government's two pronged approach of security and development, there is a need to identify areas where development work can go ahead with minimal requirement of security and those areas where security aspects will lead development. Therefore, there will primarily be two kinds of areas:-

- Areas where development will lead security aspects.

- Areas where security requirements will lead development aspects.

Development to Lead Security. Those areas where the Maoists have not been able to establish themselves should be turned into islands of development and the envy of the people living in the Maoist dominated areas. For achieving this, a number of review and monitoring mechanisms have been established by the Government of India in this regard. They are:-

- Standing Committee of the Chief Ministers of States concerned under the chairmanship of the Union Home Minister

- Review Group (earlier called the Task Force) under the Cabinet Secretary.

- Coordination Centre chaired by the Union Home Secretary to review and coordinate the efforts of the State Governments, where the State Governments are represented by the Chief Secretaries and the Directors General of Police.

- Task Force under the Special Secretary (Internal Security), Ministry of Home Affairs, with senior officers from the Intelligence agencies, the Central Armed Police Forces and the State Police Forces, to coordinate inter-state issues.

- Empowered Group of Officers, headed by the Member-Secretary Planning Commission, with officers from the development Ministries and the Planning Commission, to oversee effective implementation of development schemes in Left Wing Extremism affected States. [126]

Once progress and prosperity are available and visible to the masses, the government would have removed the reasons for alienating the people, winning their trust and support and successfully targeting the centre of gravity of any insurgency. The strategy of development has shown some results. As per a report 'India Human Development Report, 2011', prepared by Institute of Applied Manpower Research, the quantum of improvement in HDI in some of the poor states like Bihar, Andhra Pradesh, Chhattisgarh, Madhya Pradesh was higher than the national average.[127]To arrest the spread of Maoist ideology and in turn, the insurgency, the government must leave no stone unturned in ensuring that development is speeded up and carried out by taking into account the local population's requirements. The States must provide basic facilities initially and then then progress onto bigger projects. Development projects must include both social and economic aspects. The mechanism should ensure this is in place and that the young IAS officers working in these areas are motivated. The Maoists must not be allowed to take ownership of issues such as development and justice, which the State should be doing.

Security to Lead Development. There are 35 severely affected districts located in four fault line areas, wherein the government has very little control, and in some areas no control what so ever. These are the areas where a strong security response is required. Unless a secure environment exists, the government will not be in a position to uplift the area, address the problems of the people and bring progress and prosperity to them. The police and other security forces with their limitations have not been able to ensure governmental control. It will take a considerable amount of time for the security forces to be sufficiently trained and equipped to do so. In the other areas which are affected by the insurgency to some degree, mix of security and development would be needed. Sufficient security has to be provided to ensure development.

On the basis of material gathered from captured left-wing extremists, it is unequivocally clear that their objective is the violent overthrow of the Indian state and that their basic ideology is a complete rejection of parliamentary democracy as enshrined in the Indian Constitution.[128] They have spread terror and ensured that the developmental activities are obstructed. The tribal cause, which the Naxals espouse, is only a mask to further their own agenda of waging war against the Union of India. The government must reassess the law and order problem and its security response to guarantee the success of the development action plan and strike at the heart of the Maoists by regaining control of the 35 Districts presently under their (Maoists) control. Their leadership must be targeted and they must not be allowed to regroup by moving to neighbouring areas, as the case was when they were driven out of Andhra Pradesh by the Grey Hound forces. The government has two options, which are:[129]

Option 1: The Para-military forces continue to take the lead in combatting the insurgency, with assistance from the army in terms of training and guidance on counterinsurgency issues.

As per the Report of the Thirty Second Standing Committee on Defence (2008-2009), internal security duties are to be handled by Central Para Military Forces, Central Reserve Police Force and the State Police Forces.[130] Accordingly, the CRPF has been given the responsibility of conducting counterinsurgency operations. It is a large force with 220 Battalions.[131] The basic role of the CRPF is to assist the State/Union Territories in Police operations to maintain law and order and contain insurgency. Accordingly, a large number of CRPF battalions have been deployed in insurgency affected areas. Problems of training are being overcome with the setting up of new training institutions and with the experience gained by its troops in such operations.

The Indian Army with its tremendous combat experience has been assisting in training the para-military forces and State police in improving their tactics and combat capability. The Army has:[132]

- Provided pre-induction training to police and para-military forces prior to induction in anti naxal operations.

- Trained security forces to detect mines and IEDs and de-mining techniques.

- Deputed army officers to assist in training the security forces and to 'train the trainers' in counter-insurgency and jungle warfare schools run by the State governments.

- Accepted the attachment of young officers from the para-military forces with infantry battalions of the Army to facilitate in improving the quality of junior leadership and combat experience.

The CRPF battalions deployed in anti naxal operations must be re-organised so that they are composed of troops which have undergone counterinsurgency training. Further, battalion level training should be carried out to make it a more cohesive group.[133] The grey areas of intelligence, leadership and morale once addressed by the CRPF would ensure that this force is capable in subduing the insurgency.

Option 2: The Army is given the lead role in combatting the insurgency, supported by the para-military forces.

The army is mandated to primarily guard the external borders of India. Article 355 of the Constitution of India 1949 states, *"It is the duty of the Union, to protect States against external aggression and internal disturbances. It shall be the duty of the Union to protect every State against external aggression and internal disturbance and to ensure that the governance of every State is carried on in accordance with the provisions of this Constitution."* Further, Seventh Schedule (Article 246) List I—Union List, empowers the Central Government to deploy *"any armed force of the Union or any other force subject to the control of the Union or any contingent or unit thereof in any State in aid of the civil power."*

The Indian Army is one of the most well trained and experienced armies of the world in counterinsurgency warfare. They are disciplined and are led by highly capable young, motivated, disciplined, physically fit and well trained leaders, right down to the basic fighting formation. This field level leadership can ensure that only adequate force is applied in bringing the situation under control, thereby ensuring that collateral damage is reduced to the minimum. It must be remembered that there will be some levels of civilian casualties and this surgical procedure will never be painless.

Though there are provisions available to deploy the Army, committing it at present to internal security duties will stretch the Army and dilute its defence preparedness. The Army is already combating the insurgency in J&K and Assam. However, these are Border States and a peaceful internal situation is very important to be maintained in these States. Any act of aggression by our neighbours will give the Maoists ample opportunity to exploit the internal situation. India must ensure that there is no chance of a misadventure on part of our neighbours due to the lack of the state of our border defences. A solution may be to raise additional Divisions. Though the Indian Army is raising four new Divisions, they are part of a military modernisation and Army up-gradation plan in the North East region, to address the threat from China.[134] India is planning to increase the strength of her forces by almost one lakh soldiers over the next five years. Hence, the Indian Army would be hard pressed to be involved in the insurgency. It is up to the government to choose the best option - to let the CRPF which is mandated for counterinsurgency operations, continue to be the main force combatting the insurgency with assistance from the Army; or to bring in the Army to put down the insurgency at the cost of compromising the security of India's borders.

Endnotes

1   Gupta Akhil. Revolution in Telangana 1946-1951. South Asia Bulletin Vol IV No 1 Spring 1984. http://www.etelangana.org/books/revolution_tg_1946-51.pdf. Assessed on 23 April 2012.

2   Kujur Rajat. Naxalite Movement in India: A Profile. IPCS Research Paper September 2008. p-2. http://www.ipcs.org/pdf_file/issue/848082154RP15-Kujur-Naxal.pdf. Assessed on 23 April 2012.

3   Guptas .Op. Cit.

4   Bakshi GD. Left Wing Extremisim in India:Context, Implications and Response Options. Manekshaw Paper 9, 2009. Centre for Land Warfare Studies, New Delhi. p-19. http://www.claws.in/index.php?action=Claws%20 Paper. Assessed on 01 May 2012.

5   Chakrabarty Bidyut and Kujur Rajat Kumar. Maoism in India. Routledge. p- 47.

6   Left Wing Extremist Groups. http://satp.org/satporgtp/countries/india/ terroristoutfits/CPI_M.htm. Assessed on 24 April 2012.

7   The states of Andhra Pradesh, Jharkhand, Chattisgarh, Himachal Pradesh, Madhya Pradesh, Gujrat, Maharashtra, Orissa and Rajasthan have certain districts earmarked as Scheduled Areas.

8   The Fifth Schedule (FS) of the Constitution provides the basic frame for administration of the SA. The Governor is solely responsible with ultimate authority of administrating the SA, enjoying limitless powers under Para 5 of the FS this purpose. Thus, the FS is fully equipped for the protection and advancement of the tribal people. The FS has not been implemented by the Governors. The adaptation of the Panchayat Acts has been pursued by the States in a routine manner and the PESA has not been implemented in the desired manner. Madhya Pradesh, including Chhattisgarh, imitated its implementation but abandoned it hallway. The Central Government has also not pursued the matter. Andhra Pradesh has adopted the safe strategy of writing down everything mandated by PESA in its amendment to the State's Panchayat Raj Act, with the riders 'to such extent and in such manner as may be prescribed', and has left what is to be prescribed, so that the whip is finally in its rule-making pocket.

9   Narayan S. Socio-economic Roots of Maoisim Post 1980. Article in More Than Maoist. Edited by Jeffrey Robin, Sen Ronjoy, Pratima Singh. Manohar Publications, New Delhi. p-146.

10   Development Challenges in Extremist Affected Areas, Report of an Expert Group to the Planning Commission of India. p -7. http://planningcommission. nic.in/reports/publications/rep_dce.pdf. Assessed on 23 May 2012.

11   Left Wing Extremist Groups. http://satp.org/satporgtp/countries/india/ terroristoutfits/CPI_M.htm. Assessed on 24 April 2012

12   Annual Report of the Ministry of Home Affairs, Government of India, 2010-2011. p-21.

13   As per the writings of Mao Tse Tung in Selected Works, Volume 2, chapter VI.,

base areas are strategic bases on which the guerrilla forces rely in performing their strategic tasks and achieving the object of preserving and expanding themselves and destroying and driving out the enemy. Three pre-conditions for building a base area firstly are creating an army, secondly defeating the security forces in these areas and ensuring insurgent control and thirdly, ensuring the support of the people by ideology and organising them for the armed struggle. http://www.marxists.org/reference/archive/mao/selected-works/volume-2/mswv2_08.htm#p6. Assessed on 02 April 2012.

14   Guerrilla zones are areas where the insurgents are trying to gain control by carrying out guerrilla warfare. The guerrilla zones are not totally under the control of the insurgents or the government forces. Such guerrilla zones will be transformed into base areas when they have gone through the necessary processes of guerrilla warfare, that is, when large numbers of security forces have been defeated.

15   Ramachandran Sudhir. The Maoist Conflict in Dandakaranya, article in The Naxal Threat: Causes, State Responce and Consequences. Edited by Raghavan VR.Vij Books, New Delhi.p-54.

16   As per Mao Tse Tung's writings on 'Protracted War', there are three stages of such a war. The first stage covers the period of the government's strategic offensive and the insurgent's strategic defensive. In this stage the form of fighting will primarily mobile be warfare, supplemented by guerrilla and positional warfare. The second stage will be the period of the security forces' strategic consolidation and the insurgents' preparation for the counter-offensive. The second stage may be termed one of strategic stalemate. The third stage will be the period of the insurgents' strategic counter-offensive and the security forces' strategic retreat. http://www.marxists.org/reference/archive/mao/selected-works/volume-2/mswv2_09.htm#p7. Assessed 0n 02 April 2012.

17   The Indian Express. 06 July 2010. http://www.indianexpress.com/news/antinaxalite-strategy-slowly-yielding-results-pillai/642921/0. Assessed on 26 April 2012.

18   Ministry of Home Affairs, Naxal Management Division letter No-II-18015/100/2011-NM/ANO dated 20January 2012. This letter is a reply to a RTI asking for information on districts affected by LWE. A list of affected districts and states forms a part of the letter. http://www.satp.org/satporgtp/countries/india/maoist/data_sheets/2008-2011.pdf. Assessed on 26 April 2012.

19   Vira Varun. Counterinsurgency in India. The Small Wars Journal, Journal article 07 December 2001. http://smallwarsjournal.com/jrnl/art/counterinsurgency-in-india-the-maoists Assessed on 26 April 2012.

20   Annual Report of the Ministry of Home Affairs, Government of India, 2010-
     2011. p-30. http://mha.nic.in/pdfs/AR(E)1112.pdf. Assessed on 26 April 2012.

21   Assam Timeline 2012. South Asian Terrorism Portal. http://www.satp.org/
     satporgtp/countries/india/states/assam/timelines/index.html. Assessed on 26
     April 2012.

22   The Times of India 14 December 2011. http://articles.timesofindia.indiatimes.
     com/2011-12-14/india/30515500_1_maoists-industrial-areas-industrial-units.
     Assessed on 26 April 2012.

23   Ministry of Home Affairs, Government of India, Annual Report 2010-2011.
     p- 22.

24   Left Wing Extremism:. An Internal Security Challenge and Response Strategy
     for Security Forces – 2015. A report prepared by Centre for Land Warfare
     Studies, New Delhi. p-10.

25   Strategy & Tactics of the Indian Revolution. http://www.satp.org/satporgtp/
     countries/india/maoist/documents/papers/strategy.htm. Assessed on 07 May
     2012.

26   Gill KPS. Trajectory of the Maoist Movement. Article in The Naxal Challenge:
     Causes, Linkages and Policy Options. Edited by PV Ramana. Pearson
     Longman. p- 15. As per figures given in this article, the strength of armed cadres
     is 8,000 men and women. The militia consists of 15,000 armed villagers who
     lead a normal life but are ready to swerve when the occasion demands. The
     project report prepared by CLAWS gives a figure of 9,000 to 12,000 cadres
     who are grouped into Companies, Platoons and Special Squads. The strength
     of a Company could vary between 60 to 100 personnel. Gen GD Bakshi (Retd)
     in the Manekshaw Paper titled Left Wing Extremisim in India, quotes a figure
     of 10,000 armed cadres.

27   Mishra JK. Theorotical and Growth Perspectives. The Indian Police Journal
     Vol. LV-No.4 October-December, 2008. p- 64.

28   Left Wing Extremism, CLAWS Report: op.cit. p- 103.

29   Bakshi. Op.cit. p-24. As per Ben West in his article Tracking the Pakistani
     Origins of Naxalite Maoist Terror in India, Indian media reports quote a figure
     of 20,000 weapons, which works out to be an average of two weapons per
     cadre. Available on http://www.thecuttingedgenews.com/index.php?article=2
     1821&pageid=20&pagename=. Assessed on 08 May 2012.

30   Bhosle RK. India: Security Scope 2006 The New Great Game. Google-Books.
     p- 56. http://books.google.co.in/books?id=0e5zQ8jrYlYC&pg=PA56&lpg=PA
     56&dq=naxal+obtain++ak-47+arms+from+ltte&source=bl&ots=iBVkWA1U

3s&sig=MuWVEgiymCNvTpfEbX35Ym1PJoQ&hl=en&sa=X&ei=YKqoT-iQKnp6ynAg&sqi=2&ved=0CHAQ6AEwAQ#v=onepage&q=naxal%20obtain%20%20ak-47%20arms%20from%20ltte&f=false. Assessed on 08 May 2012.

31   On 15 February 2008, around 500 Maoist cadres attacked the Police Training School (PTS), the District armoury and District Police station in coordinated attacks near Daspalla in the Nayagarh District of Orissa. http://www.satp.org/satporgtp/countries/india/maoist/timelines/2008.htm#orissa. Assessed on 08 May 2012.

32   Sethi Aman. Troop fatality figures show changing Maoist strategy. The Hindu, 04 April 2010. http://www.thehindu.com/opinion/op-ed/article388033.ece. Assessed on 08 May 2012.

33   Ministry of Home Affairs. FAQ.

34   Chakravarti Sudeep. Red Sun. Penguin Books. p-130. The report prepared by CLAWS also substantiates this. This report mentions that ex-servicemen may be involved in writing their training manuals

35   ANF finds first live Naxal-training camp. Times of India, 12 March 2012. http://timesofindia.indiatimes.com/city/mangalore/anf-finds-first-live-naxal/training-camp/articleshow/12227056.cms Assessed on 09 May 2012.

36   Left Wing Extremisim. Op.cit pp-114-115.

37   Mamoona Ali Kazmi. Naxalism: An Underestimated Challenge. http://www.lankaweb.com/news/items/2009/09/15/naxalism-an-underestimated-challenge/. Assessed on 07 December 2012.

38   Left Wing Extremisim, CLAWS Report. Op.cit p-115.

39   Ibid. pp-114-115.

40   Aerial route blocked? Maoists are trained to blunt air strikes. DNA 12 April 2010. http://www.dnaindia.com/india/report_aerial-route-blocked-maoists-are-trained-to-blunt-air-strikes_1370308 Assessed on 10 May 2012.. An e-book version of this book is available on http://ebookee.org/Guerrilla-air-defense-Antiaircraft-weapons-and-techniques-for-guerrilla-forces_409909.html.

41   In 2009, there were two separate incidents when IAF helicopters being utilised in election duties were fired at by the Maoists. In the first incident, a sergeant was shot in the head when the Maoist fired using AK-47 machine guns. Unconfirmed reports also indicate that there at least two more unreported incidents where-in Air Force helicopters were shot at in 2011. In April 2012, maoist have been successful in shooting a civil Dhruv helicopter given to the

Jharkhand government for anti naxal operations.

42   Naxals get training to counter aerial strikes. Deccan Chronicle, 28 April 2011. http://www.deccanchronicle.com/channels/cities/hyderabad/naxals-get-training-counter-aerial-strikes-720. Assessed on 10 May 2012.

43   Naxal Intelligence. The Asian Age, April 2012. http://www.asianage.com/india/naxals-have-own-intel-network-030. Assessed on 11 May 2012.

44   Maoist publications.

45   Singh Rakesh Kumar. Analysis of Operational Strength of LWEs. Indian Police Journal volume LVI, No 3, July-September 2009. p-10.

46   Left Wing Extremism,CLAWS report. Op.cit. p- 109.

47   Raman B. Greyhounds Ambushed. http://www.outlookindia.com/article.aspx?237823. Assessed on 11 May 2012.

48   Maoist guerrillas deliver deadliest blow to the notorious anti-Naxal elite Greyhounds. CPI (Maoist) Information Bulletin 20 July 2008. http://www.bannedthought.net/India/CPIMIB/MIB-03.pdf. Assessed 11 May 2012.

49   There is credence to what they say about their planning in this piece of propaganda. As per a newspaper report in the internet, the Greyhounds had been on an anti-maoist operation for the last three days without success. While returning to their camp, they took a short cut of crossing the Balimela reservoir in Malkangiri district of the Orissa-Andhra boarder. The naxals had taken positions on the adjacent hillocks and were able to target the Greyhounds, inflicting heavy casualties..

50   Left Wing Extremism, CLAWS report. Op.cit.p-114.

51   Ibid. pp-108-113.

52   ibid. p- 109. This is the view of Brig KS Dalal (Retd), who is employed by the CRPF in training matters.

53   Sahani Ajai. Maoists: Creeping Malignancy. South Asia Intelligence Review. Weekly Assessments & Briefings, Volume 5, No. 51, July 2, 2007. http://www.satp.org/satporgtp/sair/Archives/5_51.htm#assessment1. Assessed on 28 March 2012.

54   Left-Wing Extremist Attacks Involving People's Militia 2004-2012. http://www.satp.org/satporgtp/countries/india/maoist/data_sheets/militiaattack.htm. Assessed on 14 May 2012.

55   http://www.satp.org/satporgtp/countries/india/maoist/documents/papers/

Functioning.htm. Assessed on 14 May 2012.

56   On 04 July 2006, the Maoists carried out an attack on a CRPF and a police camp in Jhumra Pahar forests on the borders of Hazaribagh and Bokaro districts. As per a handout distributed to the locals after the attack, the raid was "Under the direction of the Central Military Commission and under the leadership of the Bihar-Jharkhand Special Area Military Commission." http://www.nchro. org/index.php?option=com_content&view=article&id=4046:naxalites-claim-armoury-loot-a-heroic-act&catid=32:armed-conflicts&Itemid=9. Assessed on 14 May 2012.

57   Left Wing Extremism, CLAWS Report. Op.cit. p-109.

58   Ibid p-111.

59   Left-Wing Extremist Attacks Involving People's Militia 2004-2012. http:// www.satp.org/satporgtp/countries/india/maoist/data_sheets/militiaattack.htm. Assessed on 14 May 2012.

60   Maoist Information Bulletin – 22, January – June 2011. p-30. http://www. bannedthought.net/India/CPIMIB/MIB-22.pdf

61   Left Wing Extremism CLAWS Report. Op.cit. p- 112.

62   Ministry of Home Affairs, Government of India, Naxal Management Division. Frequently Asked Questions. http://mha.nic.in/uniquepage.asp?Id_Pk=540. Assessed on 08 December 2012.

63   Left Wing Extremism, CLAWS Report. Op.cit. p- 112.

64   IED models to be employed for study at CRPF lab. Business Line 25 February 2012. http://www.thehindubusinessline.com/industry-and-economy/economy/ article2931434.ece. Assessed on 21 May 2012.

65   Left Wing Extremism, CLAWS Report. Op.cit. p- 113.

66   Government of India, Ministry of Home Affairs Annual Report 2010-2011. pp-20-2. http://mha.nic.in/pdfs/AR(E)1011.pdf. Assessed on 21 May 2012.

67   Chakravarti op.cit. p-88.

68   Ministry of Home Affairs, Government of India, Naxal Management Division. Frequently Asked Questions. Op.cit

69   Ministry of Home Affairs, Government of India , Annual Report 2011-12. p- 32. http://mha.nic.in/pdfs/AR(E)1011.pdf. Assessed on 02 May 2012.

70   Development Challenges in Extremist Affected States. Report of an Expert Group to the Planning Commission, Government of India, New Delhi 2008.

p- 57. http://planningcommission.nic.in/reports/publications/rep_dce.pdf. Assessed on 01 May 2012.

71   MHA Annual Report 2010-2011.op.cit. p-20. http://mha.nic.in/pdfs/ AR(E)1011.pdf. Assessed on 19 March 2012.

72   ibid. p-4.

73   Ministry of Home Affairs, Government of India, Naxal Management Division. http://mha.nic.in/uniquepage.asp?Id_Pk=540. Assessed on 19 March 2012.

74   MHA Annual Report 2010-2011. Op.cit. p-22.

75   Swami Praveen. India's Counterinsurgency Conundrum. The Hindu 23 July 2010. http://www.thehindu.com/opinion/lead/article528762.ece. Assessed on 24 March 2012.

76   MHA Annual Report 2011-12. Op.cit. p- 34.

77   Ministry of Home Affairs, Government of India. Naxal Management Division. http://mha.nic.in/uniquepage.asp?Id_Pk=540. Assessed on 21 March 2012.

78   MHA Annual Report 2011-12. Op.cit. pp-31-38.

79   ibid. p-21.

80   Naxal Management Division. Op.cit.

81   Chari PR. Countering the Naxalites: Deploying the Armed Forces. IPCR New Delhi. p-4. www.ipcs.org/pdf_file/issue/SR89-PR_chari.pdf. Assessed on 03 May 2012.

82   Chattisgarh Flounders on Road Map for Naxal Hit States. Hindustan Times 19 March 2012. p-8.

83   Ibid. p-8

84   India's Anti-Maoist Operations: Where Are The Special Forces? Eurasia Review. http://www.eurasiareview.com/05012011-india%E2%80%99s-anti-maoist-operations-where-are-the-special-forces/. Assessed on 04 May 2012.

85   Vira Varun. Counterinsurgency in India: The Maoists. Small Wars Journal. 07 December 2011. http://smallwarsjournal.com/jrnl/art/counterinsurgency-in-india-the-maoists. Assessed on 04 May 2012.

86   Swami Praveen. India's counter-insurgency Conundrum. The Hindu, 23 July 2010. http://www.thehindu.com/opinion/lead/article528762.ece. Assessed 0n 04 May 2012.

87   Press Information Bureau, Government of India Press Releas 15 September

2011. http://pib.nic.in/newsite/erelease.aspx?relid=75982. Assessed on 02 May 2012.

88   Corum S James & Johnson R Wray. Airpower inSmall Wars Fighting Insurgents and Terrorists. Kansas University Press. p-345.

89   Bakshi GD. Left Wing Extremism in India: Context, Implications and Response Options. Manekshaw Paper No 9, 2009. Centre for Land Warfare Studies New Delhi. www.claws.in/download.php?. Assessed on 01 May 2012.

90   Swami. Op.cit.

91   India's Anti-Maoist Operations: Where are the Special Forces. Eurasia Review. http://www.eurasiareview.com/05012011-india%E2%80%99s-anti-maoist-operations-where-are-the-special-forces/. Assessed on 24 March 2012.

92   Counterinsurgency Warfare School in Bastar. Navhind Times 30 October 2011. http://www.navhindtimes.in/india-news/counter-insurgency-warfare-school-bastar-army. Assessed on 22 March 2012.

93   5,000 Hard-core Maoists with Armed Militia in Chhattisgarh. Rediff News, 08 April 2010. http://news.rediff.com/report/2010/apr/08/chhattisgarh-igp-on-the-naxalites.htm. Assessed on 21 March 2012.

94   Bharat Rakshak. http://forums.bharat-rakshak.com/viewtopic.php?p=1201360. Assessed on 27 March 2012.

95   Counter Insurgency and Anti-Terrorism Schools. Press Information Bureau. Ministry of Home Affairs 09 May 2012. http://pib.nic.in/newsite/erelease. aspx?relid=83404. Assessed on 10 May 2012.

96   Bhavna Vij Arora. Armed and Dangerous. India Today. 25 April 2011. http:// indiatoday.intoday.in/story/ministry-of-home-affairs-report-country-losing-war-against-naxals/1/135349.html. Assessed on 21 March 2012.

97   Jharkand Ex-Cop Suggests Measures against Naxals. http://zeenews.india.com/ news/jharkhand/jharkhand-ex-cops-suggest-measures-against-naxals_758757. html. Assessed on 21 March 2012.

98   Routray Bibhu Prasad. Do our forces know their briefs in the Naxal heartland?. Centre for Land Warfare Studies, Article No 1935 28 August 2011. http://claws. in/index.php?action=master&task=936&u_id=155. Assessed on 28 March 2012.

99   Jha Om Shankar. Combatting Left Wing Extremism is Police Training Lacking. Occasional Paper No 3 IDSA June 2009. p- 3.

100 Andhra Pradesh Police Department. The Elite Commando Force.http://

apstatepolice.org/APPW/jsp/userunits.do?method=viewUnits. Assessed on 21 March 2012.

101 Achutan KJ. Tackling Maoists: The Andhra Paradigm. Indian Defence Review Vol 25 April 2010. http://www.indiandefencereview.com/homeland-security/ Tackling-Maoists--the-andhra-paradigm-.html. Assessed on 21 March 2012.

102 (Data sourced from Ministry of Home Affairs, Government of India, Annual Reports. http://mha.nic.in/uniquepage.asp?Id_Pk=288. Assessed on 24 March 2012.

103 AP Government to Beef Up Greyhound Strength. Oneindia News. http://news. oneindia.in/2008/07/04/ap-govt-to-beef-up-greyhounds-strength-1215189129. html. Assessed on 21 March 2012.

104 Andhra Pradesh Police Department. Op.cit.

105 Achutan. Op. cit.

106 Jha Shankar Om.Combatting Left Wing Extremism. Is Police Training Lacking. IDSA Occasional Paper 3 June 2009. p-28.

107 Mohan Vishwa. Centre looking into MPVs' vulnerability in anti-Naxal war. The Times of India 24 January 2012. http://articles.timesofindia.indiatimes. com/2012-01-24/india/30658663_1_mpvs-naxal-violence-naxal-problem. Assessed on 24 March 2012.

108 Sharma Rajnish. CoBRA Not Able To Bight Naxals. The Asian Age, 27 February 2012. http://www.asianage.com/india/mha-worried-over-futile-cobra-ops-838. Assessed on 27 March 2012.

109 The Killing Lack of Intelligence in Dantewada. Express India, 07 July 2010. http://www.expressindia.com/latest-news/The-killing-lack-of-intelligence-in-Dantewada/643182/#. Assessed on 27 March 2010.

110 Myth, Mystrey, Command Respect and Fear. http://parthsarthi.wordpress. com/tag/jharkhand-anti-naxal-operations/. Assessed on 27 March 2012.

111 Saffron terrorism' involved in many blasts: Chidambaram. Times of India, 25 August 2010. http://articles.timesofindia.indiatimes.com/2010-08-25/ india/28293975_1_saffron-terrorism-bomb-blasts-home-minister. Assessed on 04 May 2012.

112 Bring Intl Based Approach to Combat Maoist: PC to CRPF. Deccan Herald 08 February 2012. http://www.deccanherald.com/content/225543/bring-intel-based-approach-combat.html. Assessed on 27 March 2012.

113 Ibid.

114 Athale Anil. Counterinsurgency and the Quest for Peace. Vij Books India Pvt Ltd. p-181.

115 Chidu not happy with Maha anti-naxal ops. Crime Reporters' Guide. 01 January 2012. http://www.crimereportersguide.com/2012/01/chidambaram-not-happy-with-maha-anti.html. Assessed on 27 March 2012.

116 Kumar Manan. Attack on CRPF part of Maoist counter-offensive. DNA 28 March 2012. http://www.dnaindia.com/india/report_attack-on-crpf-part-of-maoist-counter-offensive_1668299. Assessed on 28 March 2012.

117 Swami Praveen. Op.cit.

118 Lack of vision affecting anti-Naxal operations in Chhattisgarh. DNA, 16 November 2011. http://www.dnaindia.com/india/report_lack-of-vision-affecting-anti-naxal-operations-in-chhattisgarh_1613453. Assessed on 04 May 2012.

119 Bringing On The Army Against The Naxals Will Be A Disaster. http://www.tehelka.com/story_main45.asp?filename=Ne120610bringing_on.asp. Assessed on 07 May 2012. EN Rammohan, is a former Director General of the BSF and has fought insurgencies in Kashmir and the Northeast. He was chosen by the Home Minister, Mr P Chidambaram to probe the Dantewada massacre of CRPF jawans by Naxals.

120 Bandopadhyay Sabyasachi. Living in a place 'unfit for humans', a battalion revolts. Indian Express 25 September 2011. http://revolutionaryfrontlines.wordpress.com/2011/09/24/india-among-the-warriors-of-operation-green-hunt-low-morale-and-growing-revolt/. Assessed on 28 March 2012.

121 Ibid.

122 Ibid.

123 Indian Military News. http://indianmilitarynews.wordpress.com/tag/suicide/. Assessed on 28 March 2012.

124 Tiwary Deeptiman. Lack of Leave, Long Hours Cause Attrition. Times of India. 22 October 2012.

125 Routray Bibhu Prasad. Do our forces know their briefs in the Naxal heartland? http://claws.in/index.php?action=master&task=936&u_id=155. Assessd on 28 March 2012.

126 Ministry of Home Affairs, Naxal Management Division. http://mha.nic.in/uniquepage.asp?Id_Pk=540. Assessed on 04 June 2012.

127 http://currentaffairsappsc.blogspot.in/2011/10/india-human-development-

report-2011.html. Asssessed on 04 June 2012.

128 Jairam Ramesh's speech on Naxalism. Sardar Patel Memorial Lecture organised by Prasar Bharati, New Delhi, October 11th, 2011. http://pib.nic. in/newsite/erelease.aspx?relid=76575. Assessed on 24 May 2012.

129 Left Wing Extremism CLAWS Report. Op.cit. p-164.

130 Report of the Standing Committee On Defence (2008-2009) (Fourteenth Lok Sabha) Ministry Of Defence. p-23. http://164.100.47.134/lsscommittee/ Defence/32nd%20Report-ATR%20Kargil.pdf. Assessed on 07 June 2012.

131 http://crpf.nic.in/crp_c.htm. Assessed on 07 June 2012.

132 Singh Rohit. Army and the Naxal Challenge. Centre for Land Warfare Studies. http://www.claws.in/index.php?action=details&m_id=1063&u_id=80. Assessed on 07 June 2012.

133 As analysed by Gurmeet Kanwal, a strategic analyst, at present, the CRPF are being employed in 'company' size formations led by inspectors with the Commanding Officer and other officers located in peace time areas. They should be employed as a cohesive battalion size formation led by experienced Commanding Officers from the front. Times of India, 28 October 2012.

134 Prepare for Peace. Purple Beret. http://www.purpleberet.com/details/wellness_ detail.aspx?id=98. Assessed on 07 June 2012.

Use Of Air Power Against The Insurgency

Insurgencies are born out of political problems and die with political solutions. How they are fought and pacified are political decisions. Accordingly, whether to use airpower in subduing the Maoist Insurgency or not is a political choice. The Home Minister of India has indicated that the government had refrained from using air power against Maoists, but the situation could change. "*At present there is no mandate to use the air force or any aircraft. But, if necessary, we will have to revisit the mandate to make some changes.*"[1]

This statement indicates that the government is considering utilising air power in pacifying the insurgency and has not ruled out an eventuality if the situation so demands. In the past, the Government of India has used offensive airpower to put down insurgencies. On 05 March 1966, the IAF was ordered to carry out strafing raids over Aizawl after Laldenga, the leader of the Mizo National Front (MNF) declared independence from the State of India. Twenty people were reportedly killed due to the airstrikes. The air strikes in Mizoram are opined to have been instrumental in checkmating the Mizo insurgents and bringing the situation under control. In the words of Gen DK Palit (Retd), "*5th March was the crucial day. At last, at 1130hrs came the air strike, IAF fighters strafing hostile positions all around the battalion area. The strafing was repeated in the afternoon... (6th March)... There was another air strike that day and that put paid to the investment. The hostiles melted away.*" By using airpower offensively, the Indian government took a difficult political decision, indicating to the insurgents that their call for independence would not be accepted.

In a more recent incident termed as 26/11, the terrorist attacks in Mumbai saw airpower being utilised in a non-kinetic role of transporting troops. There is no doubt in any one's mind that air power in non-kinetic roles can play a vital role in containing the insurgency. When the word airpower is used, 'offensive action' and the use of immense firepower by fighter aircraft in the strike role, is what comes to one's mind first. Airpower is not just about bombing and the use of direct force through the medium of air. There are many other aspects of airpower which makes it invaluable to any counterinsurgency operation. The proper application of the distinctive characteristics of air power — speed, ability to overcome physical barriers, range, flexibility, and psychological effect, when utilised in support of the ground forces, can produce significant synergetic effects. Presently, the Cabinet Committee on Security headed by the Prime Minister has cleared the use of helicopters only for casualty evacuation, troop mobility and other logistic roles. Helicopters have not been permitted to be used in the offensive role, though return fire in self defence has been authorised.

Roles for Airpower

The various roles in which airpower can be gainfully employed in supporting the ground forces in their fight against the insurgents are:-

Roles in Which Air Power is Being Employed

- Troop mobility.
- Air Maintenance/Logistics support.
- Casualty evacuation.
- Intelligence and reconnaissance roles.
- Area mapping.

Envisaged Roles

- Border and coastal patrol.
- Psychological warfare.
- Support to civil administration
- Offensive support.

Air Imperatives

Terrain. The terrain and surface conditions of the worst affected States of Bihar, Jharkhand, Odisha and Chattisgarh are described.

Bihar. The Ganges flows from the west to the east of Bihar, dividing it into two unequal parts of Bihar, i.e. the North Bihar and South Bihar. The other tributaries of the Ganges are the Son, the Budhi Gandak, the Chandan, the Orhani and the Falgu. The Central parts of Bihar have some small hills, for example the Rajgir hills, the Barabar hills, the Bateshwar hills, the Kaimur Range, the Brahmayoni hills, the Pretshila hills and the Ramshila hills. The Himalayan Mountains are to the north of Bihar, in Nepal. Bihar has notified forest area of 6,764.14 sq. km, which is 7.1 per cent of its geographical area.[2] The State has an extensive network of roads which however is generally in poor condition and quite inadequate. Bihar has 81,700 Kms of roads. Of this, 67,079 Kms are in small districts and villages. 55% of these roads are 'kutcha'.[3] Of late, the condition of the roads has started to improve with the efforts of the State administration.

Jharkhand. Jharkhand is bound by West Bengal in the east, Uttar Pradesh and Chhattisgarh in the west, Bihar in the north and Odisha in the south. It largely comprises of forest tracks of Chhotanagpur plateau and Santhal Pargana. The State has an area of 79,714 sq km of which 18,423 sq km is forest land (24%).[4] The Damodar, the Maurakshi, the Barakar, the North Koyel, the South Koyel, the Sankh, the Subarnarekha, the Kharkai, and the Ajay are the rivers in the State. The total length of roads in the State is just 4,311 km, of which 1,500 km are national highways connecting the major cities.

Odisha. The State of Odisha is bounded by the Bay of Bengal on the east; Madhya Pradesh on the west and Andhra Pradesh on the south. It has a coast line of about 450 kms and an area of 1,55,707 square kms. It has hills and mountains of the Eastern Ghats which rise abruptly and steeply in the east and slope gently to a dissected plateau in the west. The State has numerous rivers which flow into the Bay of Bengal. They are the Subarnarekha, the Brahmani, the Mahanadi, the Budhabalanga, the Baitarani, the Salandi, the Rusikulya, the Bahudu, the Vansadhara, the Nagavali, the Machkund, the Sileru, the Kolab and the Indravati. It has a dense forest cover with 37% of the State covered by forests. The forest cover is also found up to an elevation of 600 metres.

Chattisgarh. Chhattisgarh has been carved out of the State of Madhya Pradesh. It is bounded by southern Jharkhand and Odisha in the east, Madhya Pradesh and Maharashtra in the west, Uttar Pradesh and western Jharkhand in the north and Andhra Pradesh in the south. The northern and southern parts of the State are hilly, while the central part is fertile plain. Deciduous forests cover roughly 44% of the State. The total length of the roads in the State is 34,930 kms, of which 4,814 kms are district roads and 27,001 kms are rural roads.

Weather

The country experiences four distinct seasons as per the Indian Metrological Division.[5]

- **Winter.** This season starts in early December (in north-western India) and lasts till February. These months experience clear skies, fine weather, light northerly winds, low humidity and temperatures, with large daytime variations of temperature.

- **Pre-monsoon Season/ Summer Season.** The months of March, April and May make up this season. Temperatures start increasing during March and by April, the interior parts of the peninsula record mean daily temperatures of 30-35 °C. Central India becomes hot with daytime maximum temperatures reaching about 40°C at many places.

- **South-West Monsoon.** This season lasts from June till September. The monsoonal rainfall oscillates between active spells associated with widespread rains over most parts of the country and breaks with little rainfall activity over the plains. During the monsoon breaks, the weather becomes hot and humid.

- **Post-monsoon or Northeast Monsoon.** October, November

and December make up these months. During this season, Coastal Andhra Pradesh and Rayalaseema, Tamil Nadu, Kerala and South Interior Karnataka receive good rainfall. Day time temperatures start falling. Humidity starts decreasing and north and central India experience clear skies after mid-October.

The weather of areas experiencing high levels of insurgency are analysed in the subsequent paragraphs.[6] There will be a greater security response in these areas; therefore, the air effort provided in these areas will also be the maximum. Air support is greatly affected by adverse weather.

Dandakaranya Special Zone. There is not much variation in the monthly maximum temperatures in the southern part of Odisha. The temperatures vary from 28.7°C in January to 42°C in May. The hottest months are April, May and June which have an average temperature of 36°C. December and January are the coldest months with an average minimum temperature of 16°C. The monsoons set in around June and last till September. The months of July and August experience heavy rainfall, averaging 446 mm per month.

Jharkhand Fault Line. In this region there is also not much temperature variation in the south western part of Jharkhand, with maximum temperatures ranging from 24.5°C in January to 37.9°C in May. The hottest months are April and May with an average temperature of 37.5°C. December and January are the coldest months, with an average minimum temperature of 10.8°C. The monsoons set in by June and last till September. The months of July and August experience the heaviest rainfall, averaging 387.5 mm per month.

Southern Chattisgarh Fault Line. Temperatures start rising from March, where the monthly average is 35°C and peak in the month of May, when the average temperatures touch 40.5°C. April onwards, humidity starts rising and the monsoons set in by June, lasting till September. The months of July and August experience heavy rainfall, averaging 414 mm per month. Winters are mild, with December and January having an average minimum temperature of 13.2°C.

Odisha Andhra Fault Line. The coastal areas of this region have an average temperature of 31°C throughout the year, with a maximum temperature of 34°C in May. Monsoons start in June and last till October, which is also the wettest month experiencing 222.5 mm of rain. Towards the western part of this area, there is not much temperature variation throughout the year. The summer months are hotter with May experiencing an average temperature of 40.6°C. The rainfall pattern is also similar, with a difference that the maximum rainfall is experienced in the months of July and August, with an average of 273.3 mm of rain per month.

Southern Bihar Fault Line. Maximum temperatures vary from 23.3°C in January to 38.6°C in May. Winters start setting in by November, lasting till February. January is the coldest month with an average minimum temperature of 8.8°C. The monsoons set in during end June, lasting till September. July and August are the wettest months with an average rainfall of 315.9 mm of rain per month.

Effect of Weather on Air Operations. Analysis of the climatologically normalcy of the affected areas indicates that the weather throughout the year is mostly warm and humid. The month of May is hot and sultry. June onwards, the monsoons set in and rains are heavy, on nearly a daily basis. Cumulus and stratus clouds can be expected during this period.

Air operations will be affected by poor visibility, high temperatures, rainfall and clouding, especially low clouds. Poor weather conditions such as rain and strong winds limit helicopter operations. Crosswind velocities of 10-15 knots and downwind velocities above five knots will affect the selection of the direction of landing or take-off. Even on the ground, strong winds can overturn the helicopter. Heavy rain will reduce visibility, forcing the helicopter to either return to base if possible or sit down in the nearest clearing. Clouding can reduce visibility and low clouds can be dangerous, forcing the aircrew to fly lower, exposing themselves to insurgent ground fire.

Peace Time Standard Operating Procedures

Aviation is governed by strict rules and standard operating procedures written with the aim of ensuring high levels of operational safety.

Military aviation rules are also similar, especially during peace time, where flight safety takes precedence over operational requirements. However, during war, operational requirements will take precedence to a great extent, keeping flight safety aspects also in mind. At present, military aviation assets which are being utilised in the counter insurgency operations, are governed by peace time SOPs, which may appear to be restrictive.[7] Keeping in mind the operational and flight safety requirements, SOPs for counter-insurgency operations may be formulated specifically for such operations and need to be standard for all agencies.

Air Intelligence. Aircrew undertaking anti- naxal air operations need to be briefed about the current ground situation of the insurgency. This briefing would be similar to a briefing conducted by the Intelligence Officer at an IAF flying station prior to operations. The Air Intelligence Officer needs to be located at a central place where relevant inputs are available and meaningful analysis possible. While planning operations, the air intelligence officer should also be included so as to advise on aviation related inputs. A daily threat assessment would be prepared and this would be available to all aircrew participating in anti-naxal ops. In addition, relevant inputs on on-going operations need to be also provided to the aircrew so as to have the air assets suitably equipped, refuelled and manned.

Air Tasking Officer. Various agencies would require air support. These requirements need to be prioritised by the CRPF/Police element overseeing anti-naxal operations and thereafter passed on to the Air Tasking Officer (ATO). The ATO, who is an Air Force officer, should be co-located with the Air Force Task Force Commander. He will advise the security forces on air operations. On receiving requests for air support, he will study the feasibility of execution based on various inputs such as air intelligence, threat perception, Radius of Action of the helicopter and availability of air assets. This will ensure efficient tasking and maximum utilisation of scarce air assets.

Air Defence (AD) / Ground Fire Threat. The Maoists do not have an air arm and therefore there is no AD threat from them. They also do not have shoulder fired surface to air missiles as yet but could try and procure them in future. Threat to aviation assets is presently restricted to small arms fire, which has been experienced by helicopters employed in these operations. The maximum threat from ground fire is when the helicopters are in the landing and take-off phase. The Maoists have reportedly fabricated rocket launchers[8], which may be used against helicopters in the future. SOPs would have to be formulated keeping this threat in mind.

Troop Mobility

The battlefields of this insurgency are the jungles, hills and river basins found abundantly in India. Using air effort to augment and support troop mobility is best exploited when the terrain and road conditions make it difficult for surface movement. Analysis of the terrain and surface conditions of the worst affected states indicates:

- The naxals are able to utilise the thick forest cover for hiding.

- The porous borders of Bihar provide the naxals a chance to cross into Nepal and find refuge and obtain support from the Nepali Maoists.

- Road penetration in the interiors of the States is insufficient and their condition is not very good.

- River obstacles may be utilised to avoid security forces.

- The Eastern Ghats and other hilly features make surface movement difficult.

Employment

Anti-naxal operations from CRPF and police camps linked by a fixed network of roads may become a weakness. The naxals and their intelligence network will observe such facilities covertly and gather information on the schedules and routes of patrols and convoys. With this intelligence the Maoists can time their operations to avoid the security forces or plan ambushes to engage them. At present, most of the troop movement is carried out by road. A major problem is that the naxals resort to mining the roads with IEDs, exploding them to cause maximum damage and injuries. To overcome this problem, security forces have started travelling in Mine Protected Vehicles.

The Mine Protected Vehicle India (MPVI) designed and manufactured by Defence Land Systems India is a joint venture between Mahindra & Mahindra and BAE Systems. Nicknamed as '*coffins on wheels*' the Maoists have been successful in blowing up these vehicles, forcing the security forces to march on foot, thereby limiting their area of patrolling to a day's march and also exhausting them in doing so.

A large effort is also required by Road Opening Parties in sweeping the roads and clearing landmines, before opening the roads to traffic. At times, mine sweeping is of no consequence as the mines are buried up to eight feet, where the mine sweeping equipment cannot detect the IEDs. According to the revelation of an intelligence official in Raipur, an 80 Km long stretch between Sukma and Konta has been mined.[9] In May 2010, the Director General of Chhattisgarh Police Vishwa Ranjan gave an eye-opening statement that, "*Bastar region is spread over nearly 40,000 square kilometres area, of which up to 25,000 square kilometres is intensively mined.*" As per an assessment, Abujmadh in Chhattisgarh, which forms the Central Guerrilla Base Area of the Maoists, is secured by a complex system of landmines and IEDs throughout this densely forested expanse of some 4,000 square kilometres.[10] Relying on air transportation of troops would neutralise the Maoists tactics of mining roads, bridges and tracks.

Troop movement by air can also improve the reaction time of the security forces. A classic example where security forces should have been transported by air to counter a naxal attack was in April 2009. The Maoists attacked a Central Industrial Security Force (CISF) post on Damanjodi Hill in Koraput district, Orissa. An eight hour fire fight ensued without any external support. The brave security personnel did not let the post be captured by the naxals. Thirty minutes after the attack commenced, reinforcements marched 21 Km, taking six hours to reach the post, in which time nine precious lives were lost.[11] If the reinforcements had been transported by air, the naxal attack would have been thwarted much earlier, possibly without any loss of life

Another glaring example of the requirement of air transportation of troops is the Dantewade ambush. Three hours into the Maoist attack, a rescue vehicle — a modified Tata 407 known as 'bunker' that is supposedly bomb proof — started from the camp to assist the CRPF personnel. The Maoists blasted an IED and disabled the vehicle. As per the then Home Minister Mr Chidambaram the Maoists fired at and stopped rescue parties from reaching the location.[12] Helicopters were used to evacuate injured troops but were not pressed into action to reinforce the ambushed patrol.

The strategy must be to challenge the naxals on their home ground by increasing the presence of the security forces. Highly mobile small patrols are best employed to fight the naxals. Deep penetration patrols by numerous small independent squads into the jungles would achieve this. To improve their mobility, the troops would be transported into the area of interest by air and injected directly into the jungles. This would ensure that the security personnel are fresh and alert for combat and are fully equipped. These small units can also establish jungle posts subsequently increasing the presence of the security forces and making it hostile for the naxals. Transporting troops by air ensures quick response to situations by their rapid deployment and enhances their force to space ratio. A direct offshoot of this is a reduction in the number of troops that need to be deployed.

Troops can be inserted directly into the area of interest by slithering operations, landing in open areas or by para-trooping. For carrying out slithering operations, the security forces would have to be trained in such operations. For undertaking slithering operations, the helicopters need to be modified with a slithering frame. If helicopters are landed in small clearings, sufficient hard intelligence would be required regarding the safety of the landing zone and requirement of an airborne escort. Slithering is ideal for inserting a small number of troops. For larger numbers, either more helicopters would be required or they may be para dropped by fixed wing aircraft. Para operations would demand a Drop Zone (DZ) large enough for the drop. Dropping a large force permits a rapid build-up of forces. Once a large force is dropped into the theatre directly, they would be in an advantageous position to encircle the area of interest and capture their objective. Special Forces operating in small numbers can also be inserted using HALO (High Altitude Low Opening) parachutes. Special Forces inserted in this manner would have the advantage of absolute secrecy and surprise.

Advantages

Helicopters provide a measure of surprise and tactical flexibility to the Security forces. The planners can deploy and redeploy troops rapidly, something that cannot be done by road movement. Patrols need not start and end in the same place or follow the same roads and highways. A major advantage that accrues is the reduction in casualty rates caused due to IED blasts on mined roads. Providing an air bridge to the troops ensures their safe and quick deployment. This has an indirect effect of improving their morale. The second advantage is in improving the reaction timings of the security forces while responding to situations. The nature of terrain demands long enforced marches to patrol areas. Air transportation of troops to their area of patrol permits them to carry more equipment such as arms and ammunition, communication sets and rations, as they would not have to march with these loads into the jungles. This ensures a larger troop penetration in a more efficient manner. The security forces are combating the Maoists in the jungles of India. Due to the poor surface connectivity, thick forest cover and hilly tracts and the penchant of the naxals in mining existing roads, troop mobility is best carried out by air.

Air Maintenance /Logistics

An Army marches on its stomach. This saying aptly describes the importance of rations and other logistics supplies to any fighting force. A soldier with an empty stomach and gun is a recipe for disaster. As per interviews with deployed CRPF personnel, at times they have to survive on rice and tamarind juice.[13] This would have a telling effect not only on their morale but also on their health and ability to fight. The effect of morale on troops deployed in inhospitable jungle terrain and deprived of rations, is narrated very poignantly by a CRPF personal:

> *"One incident will best define how good our morale is and how powerful we feel while operating on the mined roads of Chattisgarh. We were posted in Chintalnar .There is only one bus which plies once a day. That bus was carrying ration for the whole camp. The bus starts at 6 am. Just 5 km*

before our camp, the Naxals put up a check post and took away the ration. The whole camp depended on that ration, but we couldn't do a thing. When we can't save our food, imagine the kind of morale we will be in, when it comes to saving our lives."[14]

The CRPF does not have a dedicated Supply Corps like the Army. It has to depend upon the local contractor to supply them with rations, or they resort to obtaining supplies from the local population directly. This supply chain is fraught with too many weak links, such as the availability of surplus rations with the local population, which they can provide to the security personnel; and the ability or inclination of the local contractor to deliver the rations on time. Supplying jungle out posts with rations, arms and ammunition is best achieved by air maintenance sorties. Small camps can be resupplied by helicopters. Larger camps may require supplies dropped by a fixed wing aircraft. The amount of load would dictate the choice of aircraft. This would ensure the supplies do not fall into the wrong hands and in turn help in sustaining the naxals. Similarly, mobile squads on deep penetration missions can also be maintained with supplies from the air. Airborne logistics support ensures the same task is done faster and safely, more efficiently by reducing the number of vehicles involved in the supply chain and resupplying more posts by the same air effort. Provisioning troops by air permits a freedom of movement not normally enjoyed by the security forces. The ability to rapidly supply a patrol deep in insurgent territory allows the forces to maintain pressure on the Maoists by attacking vigorously and resolutely pursuing them.

An important aspect to be borne in mind would be to ensure that air maintenance of troops and logistics support by air should not follow a set pattern. This type of air support should be randomly timed with random destinations so as to ensure that the possibility of the helicopters being targeted by the Maoists is reduced. Sufficient intelligence reports must be obtained regarding the movement of naxals in the area of air support. If intelligence inputs indicate the possibility of the presence of naxals in the area, the air effort should either be postponed or a new location for the supply chosen.

Casualty Evacuation

From 2009 to 2011, for every naxal killed, 1.24 security forces personnel were killed in subduing the insurgency.[15]Statistics indicate that the survival rate of troops injured has fallen, implying that the naxal attacks are becoming more lethal. In Chattisgarh during 2008, an injured soldier had a 56 per cent chance of survival; in 2010 his chances had been halved to 27 per cent. This implied that in 2010, 73 per cent of all soldiers injured in a Maoist attack in Chhattisgarh succumbed to their injuries.[16]When compared to the fatality rate during World War II and the Vietnam War, as per a study by the US Defence Health Board, this rate was only 19.1% and 15.8% respectively. It fell to 9.4% during Operation Enduring Freedom.[17]

The ingenuity of the Maoists in the use of IEDs has resulted in a high casualty rate, a fact reinforced by the DG (Operations) CRPF.[18]As per a study on the casualty rates of troops in Chattisgarh, from 2007 to mid-June 2011, IEDs were responsible for approximately 40% of the casualties. The survival rates of troops injured due to gunshots is also very low at around 25%.[19] Ambushes by the Naxals by first exploding IEDs and then following up with a concentrated dose of gun fire, is a tactic that they will continue to follow. Injured troops are at the mercy of the speed at which they are evacuated to the nearest medical facility. The first 60 minutes after an injury is referred to as the "golden hour." The chance of survival for critically injured security personnel depends on immediate medical aid. Prior to being evacuated by air, the injured personnel would need to be stabilised on ground. First Aid should be self administered by the injured soldier or another fellow soldier. If available, medical personnel in the team should also provide First Aid to the injured soldier. Casualty evacuation by air is probably the fastest way of ensuring that the injured personnel is transported to a facility where professional medical aid is provided within the golden hour, thus increasing the chances of survival. A medical attendant on board the helicopter could also be able to provide medical aid en-route to the hospital.

Casualty evacuation (CASEVAC) is a term used to refer to the movement of casualties aboard non-medical vehicles or aircraft from the combat zone. Normally, casualties transported in this manner do not receive en route medical care. The United States differentiates CASEVAC from Medical Evacuation (MEDEVAC) in that MEDEVAC uses a standardised and dedicated vehicle or aircraft providing en route care. Another method of transporting injured troops by air is also termed as Aeromedical Evacuation (AE) and refers to the Air Force system providing time-sensitive en route care to patients to and between medical treatment facilities.[20]There are numerous advantages of evacuating injured troops by air:-

(a) The speed with which the injured personnel can be evacuated by air to a medical facility like a field hospital or district hospital ensures the timeliness of treatment, thus contributing to:

   (i)   Saving lives.

   (ii) Reducing permanent disability.

   (iii) Increasing the number of injured personnel who can return to duty.

   (iv) Improved troop morale.

(b) Due to the characteristics of air power such as speed, range and flexibility, it is possible to evacuate patients by air over relatively long eqdistances in short periods of time. The ability of the helicopter to land in small areas or hover also makes it an ideal method of transporting injured troops from the tactical area, directly to a well-equipped hospital. Helicopters can move patients quickly over terrain where evacuation by other means would be difficult and perhaps impossible to accomplish. In turn, this does away the requirement of establishing a number of field hospitals, or first aid centres.

Most of the anti-naxal operations are carried out in thick jungle terrain. Such terrain helps the Maoist in conducting guerrilla type operations, characterised by ambushes and IED blasts. Such terrain makes evacuation by ground difficult. This is compounded with a limited road network and the possibility of being ambushed again. Hence CAEVAC by air is the best method of evacuating injured troops. While planning anti-naxal operations, Standard Operating

Procedures (SOPs) should be so formulated so as to first designate a suitable area on the map as the helipad for CASEVAC and thereafter confirm it on ground.

At times it would be difficult for the helicopter to land in the vicinity of the injured due to terrain considerations. In such cases, injured troops can be evacuated by using a Hoist or 'Forest Penetrator'.[21] While executing Hoist operations, injured troops may be evacuated during the combat situation or even after the engagement. In a combat situation, the priority would be on recovering the injured expeditiously to ensure the least possible exposure of the aerial platform to insurgent attack. These missions are high risk missions and their success hinges on an undetected approach, a quick and smooth recovery and covering fire provided by the CRPF and other security forces during departure. If the CASEVAC is performed after the combat situation and with the area sanitised by the CRPF and other security forces, the priority would be on the safety of the aircraft and patient comfort. The forest penetrator is a folding rescue seat designed for both land and water rescue operations. It is designed to penetrate thick foliage when lowered to the ground. This piece of equipment can accommodate up to three patients in a single lift.[22]

Navigating to the designated area for the CASEVAC may pose some problems in jungle terrain, where thick jungle canopy cover may make identification of en-route check points difficult. GPS equipment would overcome this problem if the troops on ground are able to relay their co-ordinates to the ground station. During CASEVAC situations, positive RT contact with the operations room would ensure the timely arrival of aid. Troops demanding CASEVAC would need to pass information on the number of troops injured and requiring immediate evacuation along with other inputs such as nature of terrain, insurgent action and availability of a landing site. This information would assist the planners in despatching a helicopter equipped accordingly.

Helicopters deployed for CASEVAC duties should be able to reach the site within an acceptable time frame. To augment their reach, a solution would be to make fuel available to the helicopter at forward locations, a concept similar to Forward Area Refuelling Points (FARPs). These FARPs could be just small clearings sufficient for permitting a helicopter to land in. The FARP could be equipped with:-

- Suitable medical facilities.
- Barrel refuelling facilities.
- Medical and technical manpower
- Radio Communication facilities.
- Sufficient security.

The advantage of these forward helipads would be:

- Increase in RoA of the helicopter.
- Flexibility of choice of helipad for subsequent refuelling.
- Increased CASEVAC cover to troops.
- Reduction in time taken for CASEVAC.
- Improved troop morale and survivability by providing them with confidence in an efficient CASEVAC and treatment system.

A prerequisite for this concept to work would be the ability of the CRPF to man and provide sufficient security to these helipads, for which detailed SOPs need to be made.[23]These helipads need not be located in remote areas but as far as possible near population centres of even village size. These FARPs could also be given a nomenclature associated with a medical facility like Forward Medical and Refuelling Area. There should be a number of them located within a grid of say 1000 Km, at a distance of 200 Km apart. In this manner, an area of 1000 km x 1000 Km is covered. If there are numerous casualties requiring repeat shuttles by the helicopter, the first lot of casualties could be off loaded at the helipad where medical support is available. The helicopter could now make repeated trips till all the casualties are recovered. Another helicopter could also be pressed into service to shuttle between the forward helipad and one of the hubs where hospital facilities are available. The CASEVAC helicopters while flying in could bring in reinforcements to help in securing the CRPF platoon which was involved in the encounter. The reinforcements would be fresh and ready for battle or hot pursuit of the insurgents.

CASEVAC is carried out during daylight hours, thus limiting this capability. A major drawback is landing at night in field conditions. The use of Night Vision Goggles (NVGs) would overcome this problem. Though some training is imparted in military aviation for night landings using NVGs, it is done in a controlled environment. Night CASEVAC is not carried out as a practice in a peace time environment, thus the capability has not been developed and perfected for undertaking during the prevalent insurgency situation. The Dhruv ALH helicopters employed by the BSF carry civil markings[24] and thus are flown by civil pilots who would not be trained at all in such operations at night.

Close Air Support missions are those missions flown in the offensive role in support of the ground forces. These missions may be Pre-planned and dovetailed with a ground operation or Immediate, where the ground forces request for offensive air support. Similarly, CASEVAC missions are also flown in support of the injured ground forces. Therefore, such missions should go into the planning stage in major thrusts against the Maoists and be termed as Pre-planned or be Immediate where an ambushed patrol requires evacuation of injured troops. The Air Intelligence Officer would be able to brief the aircrew regarding the expected threat from the Maoists.

At present our security forces do not have a dedicated aircraft for medical evacuation. A dedicated aircraft, generally helicopters, are marked with a Red Cross on a white background and are modified to carry a number of lying patients in 'litters'. The United States uses the UH-60A Blackhawk, SH-60B Seahawk, CH-46 Sea Knight and theUH-1H/V Iroquois helicopters modified with various litter configurations.[25]In India, the ONGC is reported to be contracting with Pavan Hans to modify the Dauphin multi-purpose twin-engine helicopter in this role. The helicopter will have on board all medical equipment and trained staff.[26] The HAL produced Dhruv helicopter is also capable of being modified in this role with ventilators and two stretchers.[27] Apart from helicopters being used to move casualties, seriously injured troops can be evacuated by fixed wing aircraft from small hospitals to larger ones which would be better equipped to handle serious cases.

These aircraft are equipped and staffed to stabilise the patient even in-flight. They are equipped with medical equipment such as Multi System Monitors, defibrillators, transport ventilators and other emergency equipment and drugs. The aircraft can evacuate a number of lying or sitting patients by configuring the aircraft accordingly.

Intelligence: Surveillance and Reconnaissance

Intelligence is perhaps one of the most important tools in the fight against the Maoist insurgency. As brought out in the previous chapter, the security forces are starved of actionable intelligence. In subduing the Maoist insurgency, information gathered from surveillance and reconnaissance is required to generate the intelligence needed to address the issues propelling the insurgency. At the tactical level, to be able to engage the naxals on their home ground, they first need to be identified, tracked and thereafter neutralised by hard or soft kill. For this, good, timely and authentic intelligence is essential. The local population will normally not be the people providing this information for reasons covered earlier. The naxals do not rely on current methods of communication such as mobiles or wireless. Therefore monitoring them through Signal Intelligence (SIGINT) is difficult. Though ground level intelligence is very important, a vital substitute and a major intelligence provider can be by exploiting technology via air power. One of the best ways of intelligence gathering is continuous observation from the sky. To drive home this point, the US Air Force is the largest provider of surveillance and reconnaissance to its defence forces.[28]

To reiterate, intelligence is processed data or information which is the product of collecting data from various sources, processing and integrating it and thereafter evaluating, analysing and interpreting this data to give a coherent picture.[29]Surveillance and reconnaissance refer to the means by which the data is observed. Surveillance is "systematic" observation to collect whatever data is available, while reconnaissance is a specific mission performed to obtain specific data. When these three processes are combined as Intelligence, Surveillance, and Reconnaissance (ISR), this activity can be described as an activity that co-ordinates and integrates the planning and operation of sensors, assets and the processing and dissemination systems. These sensors are both ground and air based, while the *assets* would imply intelligence operatives gathering ground intelligence.

The government has realised that human resources alone are not sufficient to counter acts of violence; technology is the key weapon in this conflict.[30] Accordingly, a technology backed approach is being adapted for gathering intelligence. For obtaining information and conducting surveillance, the medium of air and space offer an uninterrupted bird's eye view of the area of interest. With technological advancements, Unmanned Aerial Vehicles can be used to carry out continuous surveillance of suspected naxal hide outs, training camps and other areas of interest. Surveillance by these platforms can also detect unusual movement of the insurgents which can help in analysing their plan of action and prepare the security forces to respond appropriately.[31] Real time surveillance by UAVs can be indispensable in assessing whether specific locations are likely sites of Maoist activity and may be used to track the Naxals during operations. Aerial photographs can assist in planning operations and can help in detecting long term changes in existing structures, new construction or activities.

Apart from surveillance by UAV platforms, space based assets are also able to capture images of remote areas. During Operation Lalgarh[32], satellite imagery obtained from RISAT-2 helped the security forces in locating the hideouts of the Maoists and was instrumental in giving an idea of their strength.[33] One of the disadvantages in obtaining satellite imagery is the lead time normally required for asking for the imagery and the time taken for obtaining the processed information.

Area Mapping

The security forces undertaking anti-naxal operations are using some maps which are out dated and have not been updated for a considerable period of time.[34] As a result operations are incorrectly planned at the very outset, leading to wasteful effort. The security forces use Google Maps imagery to plan their operations. This imagery, though not real time, is definitely more current than some of the available maps. Updating the maps of naxal infested areas can be carried out efficiently by the use of satellite imagery. Satellite imagery can also play an important role in executing operations in remote jungle areas.[35]

On-going Air Operations

Operation Triveni. Since 20 December 2009, the IAF is undertaking Operation Triveni in support of the anti-naxal forces with troop movement, logistics support and casualty evacuation.[36] This operation was initially conceived to cover Chhattisgarh, Maharashtra and Andhra Pradesh, and has recently been broadened to include Odisha, Bengal, Jharkhand, Bihar and Madhya Pradesh.[37]

An Air Force officer of the rank of Air Commodore is designated as the Task Force Commander (TFC) of the Air Force element. He is co-located at the Headquarters of the Anti Naxal Task Force (HQ ANTF) at Raipur. Requirements for air support are given by the State Inspector General of Police. They are vetted by the TFC and accepted depending on the availability of resources and their feasibility.

BSF Air Wing. The BSF Air Wing has its bases at Raipur and Ranchi. The Air Wing Fleet consists of Embraer-135 J, Avro (HS-748) and Super King B-200 aircraft and ALH (Dhruv), Cheetah and Mi-17 1V helicopters. The BSF helicopters are also providing air support to anti-naxal forces. They are utilising Mi-17 and Dhruv helicopters. The BSF is in the process of procuring six additional Mi-17 helicopters to augment the air effort.

Hiring of Civil Helicopters. The Ministry of Home Affairs had proposed to hire 13 Mi-17 helicopters through a civil company- Global Vectra. However, these plans were shelved due to various security related issues and objections by the Director General Civil Aviation (DGCA). The MHA is now exploring the feasibility of hiring Mi-17 helicopters from another company.[38] The Bengal, Chhattisgarh and Jharkhand governments have also hired civil helicopters for counterinsurgency operations.[39] The Chhattisgarh government has hired civil registered Chetak helicopters belonging to a private company under the Non Scheduled Operator's Permit of another company.[40]

UAVs. UAVs have been deployed for gathering intelligence. There range can be increased by controlling them by satellites.[41]The

CRPF is also in the process of acquiring small UAVs for 'over the hill' capability. The police forces utilised satellite imagery for locating areas where the Maoists are cultivating poppy to fund their operations.[42]Destroying these poppy fields helps in curtailing the funding of their operations.

Drawbacks in Current Air Operations

Quantum of Air Effort. Air effort is always a scarce commodity. Air power needs to be applied in a concentrated and continuous manner to be effective and show positive results. However, figures indicate that it is definitely very limited when compared to the requirement. Till 31 March 2012, a total of 2492 hours in 3602 sorties had been flown in support of anti-naxal operations.[43] This works out to an average of just 25 hours per helicopter, per month. This paucity of air effort is magnified with the poor serviceability state of BSF helicopters. Presently, the Dhruv helicopters of the BSF have been grounded owing to various maintenance related problems, while its Mi-17 fleet of six helicopters also has a poor serviceability rate due to the unavailability of spares, which further hampers air operations.[44]Hence the employment of air power in anti-naxal operations is negligible as compared to the effort which is required. Employment of air assets is superficial. Air operations in support of the ground forces need to be continuous and be able to meet their requirements.

Realising this, the Home Ministry was ready to spend a phenomenal amount of money to hire a civil firm to provide it with air effort, using Mi-17 helicopters. As per an Expression of Interest issued by the Ministry of Home Affairs in 2010, there were plans to hire 13 Mi-17 helicopters or equivalent for operations in LWE affected States of Andhra Pradesh, Bihar, Chhattisgarh, Jharkhand, Maharashtra, Madhya Pradesh, Orissa, Uttar Pradesh and West Bengal. The helicopters were to be employed for evacuating casualties, search and rescue operations, movement of armed troops and surveillance.[45] This deal could not materialise.[46]

Infrastructure.   Anti-naxal air operations are undertaken from civil airfields. However, there are no hangars at these airfields, even though the State governments have been requested to build these hangars. Hangars are necessary for certain servicing related tasks and also to provide a secure area to park overnight. A case in point is Jagadalpur, where the state government has not yet created this infrastructure.[47] Further, Aviation Turbine Fuel[48] (ATF) should be available at forward helipads to enable flexibility of operations, which at times has not been positioned by the State authorities.[49] The forward helipads are also not built as per the correct dimensions.[50]

Security to Helipads. While transporting troops, logistics supplies or evacuating casualties, helicopters are required to land at remote helipads in naxal affected areas. In the past, IAF helicopters have been shot at by the Maoists. It is only due to the Standard Operating Procedures employed by the IAF that no helicopter has been shot down yet. The Maoists are training for firing at an airborne helicopter and they may at some point of time get proficient enough to shoot one down. Take-off and landing phases at remote helipads are the two phases most susceptible to ground fire. Though the Maoists have not fired at the helicopters with rockets yet, intelligence inputs indicate that they are in possession of a crude rocket which may be used in the future. Due to the threat from the ground, it becomes very important for the security forces to sanitise the helipads for safe air operations.

Co-ordination of Air Effort. There are three operators undertaking air operations - IAF, BSF and civil helicopters. Command and control of these helicopters is the responsibility of the operator. Tasking is done by the IG at HQ ANTF, Raipur to the three operators individually. There is no central agency co-ordinating their movement, other than the FIR Kolkata, where a Flight Plan is filed. The area of operations is Class G airspace which has no RT cover or positive ATC control with Kolkata.[51] This can result in a near miss or collision.

Search and Rescue (SAR). While undertaking military air operations, especially where there is a high probability of being shot, quick reaction SAR cover by a helicopter standing by on ground is paramount for recovering the injured and in turn bolstering the morale of all. Though an SAR organisation does exist and is well established[52], it does not cater for an immediate reaction where the aid is available within a very short period of time in a hostile environment and accordingly equipped.

Civil Aviation Issues

Training Levels of Civil Operators. The training imparted to civil pilots for obtaining a civil license is vastly different from military aircrew. Civil Aviation pilots are taught how to fly in a safe environment without any hostile enemy opposition. Training for take-off and landing, procedures for flying from one place to another and various landing phase procedures is the core training imparted to them. On the other hand, military aviators are taught in addition to all this, how to fly in a hostile environment with a high risk to their lives due to enemy action. Hence, their situational awareness is much higher, reaction to emergency situations is more controlled and correct and they also have a higher risk taking capability. Anti-naxal operations involve movement of troops, logistics support, evacuating casualties, search and rescue operations and surveillance by day and night.[53] These are definitely operations related to military aviation and not civil aviation. Other than ex-military pilots, the civil pilots flying in support of anti-naxal operations are not trained to undertake such operations. Flying under hostile conditions in which aircrew may be fired at by the Maoists, flying at times single pilot, undertaking long duration sorties and landing in remote helipads is stressful and needs specialised training.

Standard Operating Procedures. All civil operators are required to follow an approved Operational Manual. No civil operators Operational Manual will have procedures laid down for anti-naxal operations or emergency actions if fired upon by the naxals.

Insurance Cover. Civil pilots flying in these operations are risking their lives beyond their call of duty. Towards providing them with financial security in case of an eventuality, they need to be insured for an appropriate amount. It is the duty of the civil operator to do so. The operator needs to inform the insurance company about the heightened risk. Insurance policies which insure pilots for high risk situations and high amounts are expensive. Pilots have refused to fly anti-naxal operations due to very low insurance covers. One company undertaking anti-naxal operations had insured its pilots for just Rupees 15 lakhs while the cover to Pawan Hans pilots was under Rupees 30 lakhs.[54] On the other hand, insurance of military aviators is much higher. During operations, benefits which accrue to the pilots in case of an accident are also enhanced. Further, as they are part of a system, the system looks after its own. This is not the case in civil aviation.

Envisaged Roles of Air Power

Psychological Warfare. In battling past insurgencies, airpower has played an important role in influencing the minds of insurgents to surrender.[55] The government needs to be able to convince the population prejudiced by the Maoists about the hopelessness of their cause and how the Maoists are not allowing peace to return to their lands and inhibiting development. The local population needs to be educated regarding the cruelty of the Maoists and how oppressive their ideology is. The Maoist cadres need to be explained that it is just a matter of time when the naxals will be defeated and all those supporting the naxals will have to face the law of the land. These cadres are to be induced to surrender by explaining to them the way that they can do so and the benefits that will accrue to them on surrendering. They have to be convinced about being treated well after they surrender.

The Naxal Management Division of the Ministry of Home Affairs has formulated a Surrender Policy. The Surrender and Rehabilitation policy is part of the multi-pronged conflict management and resolution strategy adopted by the central government. Though this policy is well articulated and spells out the benefits that surrendered naxals will reap, this policy has not been very successful in persuading the insurgents to surrender.[56]In 2009 only 150 naxals surrendered while in 2010, this figure increased marginally to 244.[57]

Leaflets explaining the benefits of surrendering and the hopelessness of their (Maoist) cause can be dropped from the air by fixed wing aircraft or helicopters. The remoteness of the insurgency affected areas makes the medium of air ideal for distributing these leaflets over a large area. Most of the Maoist cadres may not be able to read the leaflets. To overcome this problem, loudspeaker transmitted messages can be broadcast from helicopters.[58]With the availability of small MP 3 players, these devices can be dropped with pre-recorded messages extolling the advantages of surrendering.

Psychological operations (PSYOPS) are normally understood as operations in which leaflets are dropped from the air or messages broadcasted via loudspeakers, radio or television to influence a target audience, in this case, the Maoist insurgents. There is another more profound psychological effect that air operations can have on the Maoists. This is demoralising them and impressing upon them the impotence in their fight against the government.

Air operations being conducted against the naxals are to support the ground forces in troop mobility, logistic support and casualty evacuation. If these operations were to include kinetic attacks against the Maoists, there would be an adverse effect on the morale of the naxals. In past operations, the morale and will to fight of insurgents has been severely affected when they were kept under sustained air attacks during day and night. Follow on ground operations when co-ordinated with these air operations were able to exploit the psychological effect that the air operations had created.[59] Aerial observation and precision targeting of the Maoist cadres would create the fear of the unknown and unseen. This fear may be so profound, that it would also inhibit the Maoists from firing at the helicopters being employed in the fear that they would be detected and targeted.[60] These psychological affects would only manifest if and when the political decision is taken to use offensive airpower.

Support To Civil Administration. The areas affected by the insurgency are the remote villages and areas where poor road communication creates numerous problems. As a result, these areas are neglected with hardly any governance and development, offering the ideal environment for the plague of poverty and discontentment, which feeds the insurgency. Fuelled by a spate of kidnappings by the Maoists of civil administration officials and politicians, the movement of the district officials and their staff is restricted. As a result, some State governments place constraints on the movement of these officials, while other officials avoid moving out. These abductions demoralise the officers and hampers progress further, leading to a negative spiral. Development work gets delayed. For example, in Bihar, the Indira Awaas Yojana (IAY), a housing scheme for the poor, endured a holdup as officials were reluctant to inspect the interior villages.[61] This is what the Maoists want.

To deny the Maoists the pleasure of achieving their goal of hampering development to the poor and needy, moving government officials by a safer means of air transportation is an ideal alternative. Though expensive, this is a perfect way in utilising civil helicopters. These helicopters employed in transporting civilian personnel in executing their duties would be able to adhere to the rules and regulations governing civil aviation. Places where development activities are progressing can have a helipad constructed and guarded to enable smooth movement of government officials and people involved in the various projects. Once development comes to the backward areas, progress will follow and the 'centre of gravity' of the insurgency will slowly start tilting away from the insurgents.

Border and Coastal Patrol. As per the Maoist document 'Strategy and Tactics of the Indian Revolution', the insurgents plan to develop coastal areas into Base areas and inflict *"heavy losses on the enemy"* (Indian government) by attacking coastal shipping. The coastal districts of Ganjam in Odisha, and Vishakapatnam, Prakasam, Guntur, East Godavri and Srikakulam in Andhra Pradesh are Naxal affected districts.[62] These two States also have an extensive coast line with many remote areas from where the Naxals can launch attacks on coastal shipping. At present, the Maoist insurgency has not developed to a stage where the insurgents have the capability to attack coastal shipping. But who thought that the LTTE would have their own naval and air wings. The possibility of the insurgents building up the capability to attack ships in the future should not be ruled out. Patrolling the long eastern coast line is best undertaken by aircraft. Coast Guard aircrew undertaking coastal patrols by fixed wing aircraft should be aware of the insurgents game plan and be briefed to be on the lookout for any such development.

Offensive Support. History tells us that in any counterinsurgency campaign, using offensive fire power is detrimental to the whole effort. The Maoist insurgency is considered by some as a fight of the downtrodden poor oppressed people against a government that does not do enough for their development, a fact also accepted by the central government. In combating an insurgency waged by a class of Indian society armed with weapons ranging from primitive bows and arrows to modern firearms, the use of offensive fire power through the medium of air would be viewed as excessive, cruel, unfair, unjust and uncalled for. It would generate much outcry among the public and there would be a political price to be paid. This insurgency which is steered by the ideology professed by Mao has to move through various stages, starting from guerrilla warfare and culminating in positional warfare. Offensive airpower is best employed when any insurgency has moved onto a stage where the insurgents present a well-defined target and have reached a stage of positional warfare. This stage is yet to be reached by the insurgents. Hence, employment of air launched area weapons such as bombs and rockets and destruction of villages and jungles with associated collateral damage is not required and will hopefully never be. If ever this insurgency does reach a stage of positional warfare, there would be enough reason and support for employing offensive air power in strike roles.

Technology has moved forward and weapons are being developed for use in situations where targeting requires precision, smaller blast effects and minimum collateral damage. These technological advantages presented by air power are coupled with the advantage of ensuring that the assessment of whether to use these weapons or not is under the control of highly trained and disciplined aircrew. These decisions would be well thought of without any pressures such as time and hostile fire, and be much better as compared to the use of fire power by the foot soldier who may not be as well trained and would be under pressure from hostile attack.[63] These advantages offered by airpower have not been understood and accepted by most policy makers and planners. There will be a tendency, as experienced by the Americans during Operation Enduring Freedom, to delay approving the elimination or engagement of a target through the medium of air as the ability of smart weapons to destroy the target with pinpoint accuracy and minimal collateral damage may not be appreciated.[64]

The use of offensive air power against the Maoist insurgents is a subject of much debate and even two Chiefs of Air Staff had differing views on the subject.[65] Air Chief Marshal PV Naik was of the opinion that the IAF should not be used against its own citizens and also brought out the requirement of an absolute certainty that the naxals were the enemies of India. An earlier Air Chief, however, differed and opined that armed helicopters could be useful in locating the Maoist logistic trail and destroying it.[66] He also professed well planned operations while supporting the security forces with protective aerial fire in counter ambush operations in attack and in defence. The government on its part has kept its options open for the moment and has permitted IAF helicopters to fly with machine guns and fire in self defence.

Offensive roles of air power are best limited to operations in support of the security forces. These operations should be dove tailed in the overall operational plan, leaving nothing to chance. As the term offensive air support gives a picture of aerial platforms taking the initiative, a more palatable term of 'Defensive Fire Support' should be used to describe them. Defensive Fire Support would include air support operations undertaken in support of ground forces to defend them from Naxal surprise attacks/ambushes. These close air support missions would also act as an airborne command post and provide the troops protection with fire support.

Airborne Command Post and Force Protection. This method of employing air power in support of troops was first conceived and successfully utilised in the Rhodesian War. The Rhodesians established a unified command of the army, air force and police forces. Exploiting helicopters to enhance troop mobility and act as an aerial command post was found to be very effective in fighting a guerrilla war in the jungles.[67]

In this concept, helicopters and one fixed wing aircraft are employed. The force commander employs one armed helicopter as his aerial command post. The helicopter employed in such operations should have a good field of view and should be light and manoeuvrable. The other helicopters are used to transport troops to act as a blocking force. These troops would be lightly equipped with just arms and ammunition and water bottles to enhance their mobility for a short and intense engagement. On spotting Maoist insurgents, a fixed wing aircraft will come in low and drop around twenty troops to act as a sweeping force. The force commander would get airborne in his helicopter and the other helicopters numbering around four would be directed by the force commander to drop their troops at various points to box in the insurgents and act as a blocking force.

The force commander with an elevated view will be able to direct operations and assist the troops in engaging the naxals. He would be able to identify the insurgents and appraise the troops on what the insurgents are doing. Developing this concept further, once the insurgents are spotted, the force commander can mark their position by dropping a smoke candle. In case sufficient air effort is not available for transporting the troops or the operations do not envisage the para dropping of troops, a force commander can still be launched to direct ground operations from the air.

Towards force protection, the force commander can protect the troops by providing fire support. Once the insurgents are located, aerial fire will also be able to drive them out into the open, so that they can be engaged by the troops on the ground.

Unmanned Aerial Vehicles. UAVs are classically employed to undertake dull, dirty and dangerous missions.[68] These roles cover numerous missions which were earlier carried out using conventional manned aircraft or other ground based equipment. Operational experience indicates that with their long endurance capability and resulting high loiter times, they are ideally suited for surveillance and reconnaissance roles. They have the ability of being programmed to follow a predetermined route which results in a good automatic mission capability. With the ability to transmit real time data to the operations centre, decision making is faster, resulting in short sensor to shooter cycles.

The missions in which UAVs can be employed in anti-naxal operations are:

- Reconnaissance.
- Target location and designation.
- Battle management or situation control.
- Communication and data relay.
- Digital mapping.
- Mine detection.

UAVs do suffer from some limitations. They are very easily affected by weather such as clouds, haze and smoke, rain and ice. Adverse weather limits their operations more than that of manned aircraft. Due to their slower speed, they take a long time to search a designated area, which affects surveillance and reconnaissance missions and delays extracting intelligence from such inputs. Lastly, the UAV system requires a large number of trained manpower, such as external and internal pilots, data processors and intelligence analysts.

Endnotes

1   Govt May Have to Use Air Power Against Naxals: Chidambaram. Times of India 08 April 2010. http://articles.timesofindia.indiatimes.com/2010-04-08/india/28117796_1_air-power-maoist-strike-air-force. Assessed on 14 June 2012.

2   State Profile of Bihar. http://india.gov.in/knowindia/state_uts.php?id=5. Assessed on 15 June 2012.

3   Bihar Road Sector Development. , A Report of the Special Task Force on Bihar, Planning Commission of India. pp-1-5. http://planningcommission.nic.in/aboutus/taskforce/tsk_brs.pdf. Assessed on 15 June 2012.

4   State Profile of Jharkhand. http://india.gov.in/knowindia/state_uts.php?id=12. Assessed on 15 June 2012.

5   S. D. Attri and Ajit Tyagi. Climate Profile of India. Government of India, Ministry of Earth Sciences, India Meteorological Department. pp-2 to 5. http://www.imd.gov.in/doc/climate_profile.pdf. Assessed on 08 November 2012.

6   Metrological data of the areas of Malkangiri and Gadrichiroli in the Dandakaranya Speacial Zone, Gumla in the Jharkhand Fault Line, Kanker in the Southern Chattisgarh Fault Line, Srikakulam and Khammam in Odisha Andhra Fault Line and Gaya in Southern Bihar Fault Line have been analysed. Data has been assessed from http://www.imdpune.gov.in/research/ncc/climatebulletin/bulletin_index.html.

7   In a newspaper article, the civil administration wanted IAF helicopters to violate SOPs of keeping helicopter engines running after landing at remote helipads in support of anti maoist operations. Dutta Sujjan. IAF protests 'widen red role' order. The Telegraph, 02 July 2012. http://www.telegraphindia.com/1120702/jsp/nation/story_15680803.jsp#.UJx8xi7QpF8. Assessed on 09 November 2012.

8   Nayak Deepak Kumar. Maoists: Growing Arsenal. http://www.ocnus.net/ artman2/publish/Dark_Side_4/Maoists-Growing-Arsenal.shtml. Assessed on 09 November 2012.

9   Chakravarti Sudeep. Red Sun – Travels in Naxalite Country. Penguin Books. p-86.

10   Singh Ajit Kumar. Maoists and Their Mines. http://www.indiablooms.com/ MedleyDetailsPage/medleyDetails111010a.php. Assessed on 21 June 2012.

11   Sarangi Sudhanshu. Open Up the Skies. http://www.hindustantimes.com/ News-Feed/Editorials/Open-up-the-skies/Article1-533793.aspx. Assessed on 21 June 2012.

12   Sahi Ajit. War Games People Play. Tehelka Magazine, Vol 7, Issue 15, April 17, 2010. http://www.tehelka.com/story_main44.asp?filename= Ne170410coverstory.asp. Assessed on 29 June 2012.

13   Ibid.

14   Pandey Brijesh. Hard Battles Hard Lives. Tehelka Magazine, Vol. 7, No. 29, July 24, 2010. http://www.tehelka.com/story_main46. asp?filename=Ne240710CoverStory.asp. Assessed on 29 June 2012.

15   Fatalities in Left-wing Extremism : 2005-2012 India: Year Wise Breakup. http://www.satp.org/satporgtp/countries/india/maoist/data_sheets/ fatalitiesnaxal05-11.htm. Assessed on 10 July 2012.

16   Sethi Aman. Very low survival rates of troops wounded in Chhattisgarh. http:// indianmilitarynews.wordpress.com/2011/06/. Assessed on 10 July 2012.

17   Tactical Combat Casualty Care. Defence Health Board Update, 9 March 2009. Butler Frank, MD. http://www.health.mil/dhb/downloads/Butler%20TCCC. pdf/ Assessed on 28 August 2012.

18   See note 64, chapter 4.

19   Sethi Aman. Very low survival rates of troops wounded in Chhattisgarh. http:// indianmilitarynews.wordpress.com/2011/06/. Assessed on 28 August 2912. Year on year, improvised explosive devices (IEDs) have accounted for about 40 per cent of the 624 troop casualties from 2007 to mid-June 2011. 2010 was the sole exception in which IEDs accounted for only 23 per cent of all fatalities. In 2008, an injured soldier had 70 per cent chance of surviving an IED blast; in 2010 he had only a 46 per cent chance. In the meantime, survival rates for gunshot injuries have remained steady at about 25 per cent from 2007 to 2011.

20   US Joint Publication 4-02, Health Service Support. p-I6. http://www.dtic.mil/

doctrine/new_pubs/jp4_02.pdf. Assessed on 28 August 2012.

21 The Hoist and Forest Penetrator are terminologies used by the US Army.

22 A detailed procedure of utilising the Hoist and Forest Penetrator is given in the US Army FM 8-10-6, Medical Evacuation in the Theatre of Operations, Tactics, Techniques and Procedures, Appendix E-1.

23   As per an article in the e-monthly journal Rotor India of the Rotary Wing Society of India, June 2012, the security forces have increased sanitising drills around helipads constructed deep inside jungles as the helicopters can be targeted while landing or take-off. At times these helipads are sanitised and dominated by security forces. http://www.rwsi.org/emonthly/eJune.pdf. Assessed on 31 August 2012.

24 As per the DGCA web site, the BSF have five ALH helicopters with VT markings.In December 2010, Pavan Hanshad had a contract with HAL for operation & maintenance of an additionalfour ALH Dhruv helicopters for the BSF. The Company has provided one Dhruv helicopter taken on lease from HAL to Government of Maharashtra for Anti-Naxal activities at Gadcharoli, Maharashtra..http://dgca.nic.in/aircraft/reg-ind.htm. And http://pib.nic.in/newsite/erelease.aspx?relid=79267Assessed on 31 August 2012.

25 US Army FM 8-10-6. Op.cit. p-10-34.

26 Bhaskar Utpal. ONGC to get country's first fully dedicated medevac helicopter. http://www.livemint.com/2007/12/17224603/ONGC-to-get-country8217s-fi.html. Assessed on 28 August 2012.

27 NDMA to get 12 ALHs. Deccan Herald, 20 January 2007. Assessed on 28 August 2012.

28 Chizek. J Judy. Military Transformation: Intelligence, Surveillance and Reconnaissance. Report for Congress. p-13. http://www.fas.org/irp/crs/RL31425.pdf. Assessed on 13 September 2012.

29   US Joint Publication 1-02, Department of Defence, Military and Associated Terms. p-153. http://www.dtic.mil/doctrine/new_pubs/jp1_02.pdf. Assessed on 13 September 2012.

30 Opening statement of the home minister Shri P Chidambaram at the meeting of Chief Ministers on NCTC on, 05 May2012 at New Delhi. p-3. http://mha.nic.in/pdfs/HM-OpenStat-050512.pdf. Assessed on 14 September 2012.

31 On April 11, 2009, the 57 Mountain Division of the Indian Army based in Manipur, along with the para-military Assam Rifles and State Police, launched a counter insurgency operation, codenamed 'Operation Summer Storm' against

militants of the People's Revolutionary Party of Kangleipak (PREPAK), the United National Liberation Front (UNLF) and the People's Liberation Army (PLA). The operations were well planned and numerous intelligence inputs were obtained from UAVs which monitored the camps for over a month. Routray Bibhu Prasad. Manipur: Summer Storm. South Asia Intelligence Review Weekly Assessments & Briefings Volume 7, No. 42, April 27, 2009. http://satp.org/satporgtp/sair/Archives/7_42.htm#assessment2. Assessed on 05 November 2012.

32   Lalgarh is situated in West Bengal, adjacent to the towns of Medinapore and Jhargram, approximately 50 Km North West of Kharagpur. In June 2009, this area was blockaded by the adivasis backed by the Maoists. The state government with the assistance of the centre launched Operation Lalgarh to clear the area of Maoists.

33   Mondal Pronab. Satellite Tracks Foe. The Telegraph, 27 June 2009. http://www.telegraphindia.com/1090627/jsp/bengal/story_11165932.jsp. Assessed on 29 September 2012.

34   Baweja Harinder. 30 Year Old Maps Guide Forces in Red Areas. Hindustan Times . 20 July 2012.

35   During Op Abujhmaad, the security forces used satellite imagery to plan out their operations. http://m.indianexpress.com/news/op-abujhmaad-in-a-first-crpf-enters-land-of-maoists-myths/933941/. Assessed on 06 November 2012.

36   Annual Report 2011-2012, Ministry of Defence, Government of India. pp175-176.

37   Dutta Sujan. IAF protests 'widen red role' order. The Telegraph, 02 July 2012. http://www.telegraphindia.com/1120702/jsp/nation/story_15680803.jsp#.UEV9V6mUpiN. Assessed on 04 September 2012.

38   MHA's plan to hire choppers for anti-Naxal ops on hold. The Economic Times, 07 May 2012. http://articles.economictimes.indiatimes.com/2012-05-07/news/31610422_1_anti-naxal-choppers-mi-17. Assessed on 04 September 2012.

39   Dutta Sujan. Op.cit.

40   Inputs from a pilot who flew in Chattisgarh.

41   Josy Joseph. Centre looks to deploy more UAVs in anti-Naxal fight. The Times of India, 24 Febuary 2012. http://articles.timesofindia.indiatimes.com/2012-02-24/india/31095187_1_long-endurance-anti-naxal-naxal-areas. Asessed on 04 September 2012.

42 Forces hit Maoists where it hurts – in poppy fields. The Pioneer, 11 March 2012. http://www.dailypioneer.com/state-editions/ranchi/49015-forces-hit-maoists-where-it-hurts--in-poppy-fields.html. Assessed on 04 September 2012.

43 Annual Report 2011-2012, Ministry of Defence Op.cit .p-176.

44 Par panel raps MoD for failing to service BSF's choppers. The Times of India, 06 May 2012. http://articles.timesofindia.indiatimes.com/2012-05-06/india/31596953_1_anti-naxal-mod-helicopter-fleet. Assessed on 04 September 2012.

45 The full text of the Expression of Interest is available on http://www.mha.nic.in/writereaddata/12840512591_EOI-090910.pdf.

46 Op.sit Dutta Sujan. The Home Ministry had planned to hire 13 Mi-17 helicopters on wet lease from Global Vectra at an estimated Rupees 45 crore each. This plan had to be shelved as the owner of the company was not given security clearance.

47 Dutta Sujan. Op.cit.

48 Aviation Turbine Fuel is a colourless, combustible, straight-run petroleum distillate liquid. Its principal uses are as jet engine fuel. The most common jet fuel worldwide is a kerosene-based fuel classified as JET A-1.

49 Dutta Sujan. Op.cit.

50 Inputs from aircrew.

51 In a Class G airspace, RT cover is not mandatory while flying under Visual Flight Rules. This airspace extends from ground level to 10,000 feet and is virtually uncontrolled.

52 India has evolved a Satellite-aided Search and Rescue programme participation in the COSPAS/SARSAT systems. It operates on 121.5MHz, 243MHz and 406MHz. Location accuracy is normally within 20Km on 121.5MHz and 243MHz beacons and 5Km on 406MHz beacons. The system will detect transmissions on these three frequencies throughout the India Search and Rescue Region (SRR) and also SRR of Bangladesh, Myanmar, Bhutan, Indonesia, Kenya, Malaysia, Maldives, Mauritius, Nepal, Seychelles, Singapore, Somalia, Sri Lanka, Thailand and Tanzania. Under this programme Local User Terminals (LUT) have been established at Bangalore and Lucknow. Indian Mission Control Centre (INMCC) at Bangalore is responsible for coordinating with Rescue Coordination Centres and other International mission Control Centres.The organisational set up is given in AIP 3.6.

53 These are the roles given in the EoI circulated by the Ministry of Home Affairs

for hiring helicopters.

54   Inputs from a civil pilot who undertook anti-naxal operations. The IAF
     covers its aircrew for Rupees 50 lakhs. In case of accidents during operations,
     additional benefits are also provided. Further, as a Service, the IAF looks after
     its Human Resources and their families.

55   The effect of psyops during the Malayan insurgency has been covered in the
     previous chapter.The British dropped numerous leaflets asking the insurgents
     to surrender. During the Gulf War, 29 million leaflets were dropped. These
     leaflets influenced the Iraqi soldiers to desert or surrender. Hosmer T
     Stephen. The Psychological Effects of US Air Operations in Four Wars. Rand
     Corporation.p-148. http://www.rand.org/pubs/monograph_reports/MR576.
     html. Assessed on 19 September 2012.

56   Guidelines for Surrender-cum-Rehabilitation of Naxalites in the Naxal Affected
     States. Naxal Management Division. http://mha.nic.in/pdfs/nm_pdf5.pdf.
     Assessed on 19 September 2012.. These guidelines start on a sorry bringing
     this fact out.

57   Press Information Bureau, Government of India. 01 December 2010. http://pib.
     nic.in/newsite/erelease.aspx?relid=67973. Assessed on 19 September 2012.

58   This was successfully done during the Gulf War. Surrender messages were
     transmitted via man-packs, vehicle and helicopter mounted equipment. Hosmer.
     op.cit.p-144.

59   Hosmer.op.cit. pp- 192 to 204. A detailed explanation of how air power in
     the kinetic role has an intangible effect on the morale and will to fight of the
     insurgents is explained in these pages. These conclusions are drawn from the
     study of past wars or anti-insurgency operations.

60   Lindblom Bruce A. Psychological Impact of Airpower. US Naval War College,
     May 1998. p-7. www.dtic.mil/docs/citations/ADA351576. Assessed on 25
     September 2012. During the Korean War, the Chinese cadres had instructed
     their soldiers not to fire against UN aircraft in the fear that they may be detected.

61   Red Road Block: High Profile Abductions Leave Officials in a Tough Spot.
     Hindustan Times, 05 May 2012. http://www.hindustantimes.com/News-Feed/
     India/Red-road-block-High-profile-abductions-leave-officials-in-a-tough-spot/
     Article1-851372.aspx. Assessed on 29 September 2012.

62   http://mha.nic.in/pdfs/LWE-aftdDist-131210.pdf. Assessed on 03 October
     2012.

63   Major General Charles J. Dunlap, Jr. Collateral Damage and Counterinsurgency
     Doctrine. Small Wars Journal.http://smallwarsjournal.com/blog/journal/docs-

temp/43-dunlap.pdf?q=mag/docs-temp/43-dunlap.pdf. Assessed on 25 August 2012.

64 Benjamin Lambeth, Air Power Against Terror: America's Conduct of Operation Enduring Freedom (Rand, 2005). p-324. http://www.rand.org/pubs/monographs/2006/RAND_MG166-1.pdf. Assessed on 25 August 2012.

65 Interview wit Nitin Gokhale, NDTV's Security & Strategic Affairs Editor. http://www.ndtv.com/article/india/iaf-undergoing-major-transformation-air-chief-to-ndtv-114743?cp. http://www.thehindu.com/news/national/iaf-chief-not-in-favour-of-air-attack-in-antimaoist-operations/article390399.ece Assessed on 05 October 2012

66 Air power against Maoists. Pragmatic Euphony. http://pragmatic.nationalinterest.in/2010/04/22/air-power-against-maoists/. Assessed on 05 October 2012.

67 Corum James and Johnson Wray. Airpower in Small Wars.University Press of Kansas. pp-297-298. For a detailed account of utilising helicopters in this concept read Wood JRT in Helicopter Warfare in Rhodesia available on http://www.rhodesia.nl/firefor2.htm. Assessed on 04 October 2012.

68 Dull missions are missions which require continuous monitoring of areas where activity may occur and other tasks which are repetitive in nature. Dirty missions involve flying throughareas which are contaminated by NBC agents. Dangerous missions are those missions which are exposed to enemy offensive action such as suppression of enemy air defenses.

Legal Aspects of Employing Air Power

The Maoist Insurgency and International Humanitarian Law

The Maoist insurgency has been called a law and order problem and to be addressed by the affected State governments with the assistance of the central government.[1] The CRPF and other security organisations are at the helm of affairs in subduing this insurgency. However, this insurgency is more than a law and order problem and appears to be more of an internal armed conflict between the government and the insurgents. The following indicators substantiate this statement:

- The geographical spread of the insurgency and existence of areas under the control of the Maoists.

- The large number of insurgents.

- The organisation structure of the PLGA.

- The weapon holdings of the insurgents.

- The frequency and number of incidents and deaths due to insurgent violence.[2]

- The large number of security forces fighting the insurgency.

- The involvement of the armed forces of the country in assisting the security forces. (The army is training the security personnel in CI operations and the IAF is also deployed in CI operations.)

- Permission given to the IAF to arm its helicopters and fire back at the insurgents in self-defence.

Conflicts are governed by a set of rules, be they internal or external conflicts. International humanitarian law is a set of rules formulated for humanitarian reasons, to minimise the effects of armed conflict.

International Humanitarian Law (IHL) is also known as the law of war or the law of armed conflict and is applicable only to armed conflict. This law does not cover internal tensions or disturbances such as isolated acts of violence. However, it distinguishes between international and non-international armed conflict. IHL is based on the four Geneva Conventions of 1949.India is a signatory to the Geneva Conventions[3] and will therefore endeavour to respect and to ensure adherence to the Conventions.

As a rule, independent States did not accept any interference in the way they dealt with their domestic affairs, including internal conflict. The principle that States must refrain from intervening in matters which international law recognises as being purely domestic was widely accepted. This acceptance is reflected in the 1945 United Nations Charter, Article 2(7) which declares, *"Nothing contained in the present Charter shall authorise the United Nations to intervene in matters which are essentially within the domestic jurisdiction of any State or shall require the Members to submit such matters to settlement under the present Charter; but this principle shall not prejudice the application of enforcement measures under Chapter VII."* Therefore, non-international armed conflicts fell outside the purview of the law of armed conflict.The reluctance of States to allow internal matters to be scrutinised by international organisations has been gradually overcome, probably due to the excessive violence and cruelty characterising many internal armed conflicts. Countries have started accepting the fact that there are some state of affairs which cannot be treated as entirely internal but are of concern to the international community also. An example is the LTTE conflict in Sri Lanka. This change in attitude has permitted non-international armed conflicts to be governed by international rules, acceptable to most countries.

In 1977, there were two additional Protocols adopted to make international humanitarian law more complete and more universal, and to adapt it better to modern conflicts. They are:

Protocol I. Protocol I deals with international armed conflicts. International armed conflict arises when one State uses armed force against another State or States.

Protocol II. Protocol II deals with non-international armed conflicts. Non-international armed conflicts, also known as internal armed conflicts, take place within the territory of a State and do not involve the armed forces of any other State. An example is the use of the State's armed forces against dissident, rebel or insurgent groups. Non-international armed conflicts or Internal Armed Conflicts can be defined as:-

> *"Armed conflict which take place in the territory of a Party between its armed forces and dissident armed forces or other organised armed groups which, under responsible command, exercise such control over a part of its territory as to enable them to carry out sustained and concerted military operations."[4]*

Protocol II unambiguously states that the Protocol "shall not apply to situations of internal disturbances and tensions, such as riots, isolated and sporadic acts of violence and other acts of a similar nature," as these are not considered to be armed conflicts.

The Maoist insurgency has a command structure which exercises control over its cadres in various parts of India and the Maoists are able to carry out sustained and concentrated military type operations[5]. Therefore, this insurgency meets all the parameters to classify it as an internal armed conflict. India has protested in the UN on including this conflict as an "armed conflict."[6]India does not want to accept the insurgency as an internal armed conflict, as by doing so, it would legitimise the insurgency in some manner and open it to international scrutiny. Even though India is not a signatory to Protocol II,[7]there are many provisions in Protocol II which are part of Customary Law[8], on which IHL is infused in.[9]As per a study, Customary International Law regulates internal armed conflicts in more detail than Protocol II does.[10]

Principles of IHL

International humanitarian law covers two areas:-

- The protection of individuals who are not, or no longer, taking part in fighting.

- Restrictions on the means of warfare, in particular the weapons and methods of warfare, such as military tactics.

Principles. IHL is based on certain principles. They are[11]:

- **Distinction between civilians and combatants.** Parties to an armed conflict must distinguish between the civilian population and combatants and between civilian objects and military objectives. Any target must be a military target. Once a military objective[12] is the target, the attack may become illegal if excessive collateral damage affecting civilians or civilian objects occurs.[13]

- **Proportionality.** A military target cannot be attacked if it causes accompanying loss of civilian life, injury to civilians, or damage to civilian objects that is excessive in relation to the anticipated military advantage of the attack.

- **Military Necessity.** The use of military force is justified only to the extent it is required to achieve a military goal. This force used must not exceed the level required to stop the threatening activity. This implies that only that much force should be used so as to bring about the submission of the enemy.[14]

- **Unnecessary Suffering or Superfluous Injuries.**[15] Weapons that cause unnecessary suffering to combatants without an increase of military advantage must not be used.

The principles of IHL as applicable to land warfare are also applicable to air warfare.[16]

The Law of Air Warfare

The medium of air was used to help armies as far back as in 1870 during the Franco-Prussian War when hot air balloons were used for aerial reconnaissance. The early years of aerial warfare were not subjected to any specific legal regulations. It was only in in 1899, when the First Hague Peace Conference adopted three Conventions and three Declarations, the first of which prohibited the launching of projectiles and explosives from balloons or by other similar new means. This restriction was temporary, lasting for five years from

04 September 1900 to 04 September 1905. In 1907, the Hague Conference renewed the Declaration on aerial warfare. The articles, in effect, were customary law and as per provisions of the conference, were applicable to only those countries which were signatories to it. Hence, during World War I, France and Germany were not affected by this Declaration as they had not signed it.

After the destruction and bombing that was experienced during World War I, governments of various countries felt that there was a requirement to restrict the use of arms during war. This led to the Washington Conference on the Limitations of Armament in 1921, aimed at limiting naval warfare and other associated subjects. This conference recommended a separate Commission on aerial warfare. The Commission met from December 1922 to February 1923 at The Hague and it prepared rules for the control of radio in time of war (part I of the report of the Commission) and rules of air warfare (part II).[17] These rules to a great extent are in harmony with the customary rules and general principles underlying treaties on the law of war on land and at sea. Despite this, they were never adopted in any legal binding form.

The developments in aerial warfare and recognition of its capability of influencing the outcome of wars hindered the implementation of any rules restricting its employment. Aerial warfare has come a long way since the Italia –Turkish war of 1911-12, when aircrafts were used to bomb ground targets and today, where armed UAVs can deliver weapons with the utmost accuracy and surprise. Airpower gradually became essential to a country's military strategy. Modern technology has brought about significant changes in the employment of airpower and with the availability of high technology weapons and aircraft, new challenges are faced in protecting civilians during conflicts.

After the hostilities experienced in Kosovo and Afghanistan, history repeated itself in creating a need to once again review and restate the Laws on Air and Missile Warfare. A Program on Humanitarian Policy and Conflict Research at Harvard University (HPCR) was initiated in 2003. On 15 May 2009, the HPCR Manual on International Law Applicable to Air and Missile Warfare was published at Berne, Switzerland.[18] This Manual is not legally binding, but the University believes that it would help countries in formulating Rules of Engagement and other military procedures on air warfare.[19] The laws of air warfare are based on customary international law (thus making them binding), and are available in various secondary sources, including the HPCR manual.[20] In addition, legal implications with respect to civil aviation assets undertaking counter-insurgency operations need to be studied by the experts.

Definitions

Combatants. Combatants are members of armed forces and dissident armed forces or other organised armed groups, or others taking an active (direct) part in hostilities. Civilians who take part in the hostilities become combatants. Medical and religious personnel of armed forces or groups, however, are not regarded as combatants and are subject to special protection unless they take an active (direct) part in hostilities.[21]

In the case of the Maoist insurgency, armed groups for the purpose of this study would mean the PLGA, its leaders and its cadres. Civilians who actively participate in the insurgency would also be called combatants.[22] Examples of active (direct) participation by the Maoists would include activities such as attacking the government forces, the government's material or facilities; sabotaging government installations, acting as members of a gun crew, delivering ammunition; or gathering intelligence in the area affected by the insurgency.

Military objectives. Military objectives are objects which by their nature, location, purpose, or use, make an effective contribution to military action and whose total or partial destruction, capture, or neutralisation, in the circumstances at the time, offers a definite military advantage.[23]

A civilian facility can become a military objective if it is used for a military purpose. Hence a hospital, church or school, or cultural object can become a military objective. 'Purpose' indicates that based on intelligence, the adversary will be using or misusing the object for a military requirement in the future.

"**Collateral damage**" means incidental loss of civilian life, injury to civilians and damage to civilian objects or other protected objects or a combination thereof, caused by an attack on a lawful target.[24]

Medical aircraft. A Medical aircraft is any aircraft permanently or temporarily designated exclusively for aerial transportation or treatment of wounded, sick, or shipwrecked persons, and/or the transport of medical personnel and medical equipment or supplies.[25]

Military Aircraft. Military aircraft means any aircraft operated by the armed forces of a State, bearing the military markings of that State; commanded by a member of the armed forces and controlled, manned or pre-programmed by a crew subject to regular armed forces discipline.[26]

Civilian Aircraft._ Civilian aircraft means any aircraft other than military or other State aircraft. "State aircraft" means any aircraft owned or used by a State serving exclusively non-commercial government functions.[27]

Practical Application

- In the Maoist insurgency, the two opposing parties are the State of India and the Maoist insurgents. Targets that can be engaged are combatants (insurgents) and military objects and civilians directly participating in the insurgency. Aerial attacks directed against civilians or civilian objects are prohibited. Whenever there is a doubt regarding whether a person is a civilian or not, he will be given the benefit of doubt and considered a civilian. A conscious effort must be made to avoid targeting civilians. Air attacks must not be carried out with the aim of terrorising the civilian population. Civilian aircrafts are not to be used for air attacks. Military aircrafts are fair targets. Hence helicopters and UAVs being employed against the Maoist insurgency can be attacked by the Maoists.

- Attacks on irrigation or water supplies, crops, live-stocks or foodstuff must not be carried out unless they are being used solely by the insurgents. If the destruction of such targets will affect the civilian population, they must not be attacked.[28]

- The weapons launched from aircraft should be capable of being aimed at a specific military target. Therefore, area weapons such as iron bombs that cannot be aimed at a specific target and are liable to cause collateral damage and injury to civilians or civilian objects without distinction; or the effects of which cannot be limited to military targets are not to be used.[29] Weapons which cause unnecessary injury and suffering to the insurgents are also prohibited. Such weapons can include Napalm and fragmentation bombs, biological and chemical weapons and blinding lasers. Herbicides are also not to be sprayed from the air in a bid to destroy foliage which may give cover and protection to the insurgents.[30]Though it is not binding that air launched weapons should be precision guided, there may be situations which demand the use of such weapons to avoid or minimise collateral damage.

- A fair opportunity must be given to care for and evacuate casualties.

- A civilian aircraft gathering information (such as aerial photography) can be attacked.[31]A civilian aircraft, if assisting in fighting the insurgency, becomes a target.

Rules of Engagement

In subduing the Maoist insurgency, airpower must be employed within legal boundaries. Thus a set of rules need to be laid out, which, airpower must restrict itself to. These rules are commonly known as 'Rules of Engagement'. These Rules of Engagement (RoE) would be based on the legal considerations covered. They may be further restrictive keeping political requirements in mind. Rules of Engagement would be mostly applicable while employing airpower in offensive roles. Some RoE that can be formulated are:

- Prior to sanctioning an aerial attack, it must be confirmed that the target is contributing to the insurgents' effort.[32] Weapons must be so chosen so as to avoid or minimise collateral damage.[33]

- No indiscriminate attack is to be carried out.

- No laser weapons meant to blind are to be used.[34]

- Whenever an aerial attack is carried out and it becomes evident that the target is not a military target, if the target turns out to be a medical/hospital or religious place; or excessive collateral damage may occur, the attack must not be carried out. Attacks on cultural property are also to be avoided unless it becomes a target of military necessity.[35] In such attacks, the civilians are to be warned of the impending attack. These warnings can be made by dropping leaflets or even through loud speakers.[36] These RoE are applicable to attacks carried out by UCAVs also.

- UCAVs may carry out attacks as long as they qualify as military aircraft. Prior to attacking, the on-board sensors must be able to distinguish between military objectives and civilian objects, as well as between civilians and combatants.[37]

- Civilians are not to be used for shielding targets. If they are still used by the Maoists, no air attack is to be carried out.[38]

- The Maoists may take refuge or utilise religious places such as temples or mosques for matters other than religion. Before attacking these holy places, it needs to be confirmed that they are being used to the advantage of the Maoists and not for prayer alone. Only on confirmation by real time hard intelligence, should such places be attacked.[39]

- The civilian population cannot be threatened with air attacks. Audio or written threats are also included in this restriction. This will not be applicable to shock and awe operations in respect of the Maoists.[40]

- Maoists who surrender are not to be attacked.[41]

- While evacuating casualties, insurgent casualties should also be evacuated without making any distinction between them and the security forces.[42]

Endnotes

1   As per the Ministry of Home Affairs, Naxal Management Division, 'Police' and 'Public Order' are State subjects. The maintenance of law and order lies primarily in the domain of the State Governments. The Central Government closely monitors the situation and supplements and coordinates their efforts in several ways. http://mha.nic.in/uniquepage.asp?Id_Pk=540. Assessed on 09 October 2012.

2   As per the Annual Report of the Ministry of Home Affairs, from 2008 to 2011, there were 7816 incidents of Maoist backed violence which resulted in 3238 deaths.

3   India signed the Geneva Conventions held on 12 August 1949 on the 16 December 1949. http://www.icrc.org/ihl.nsf/WebSign?ReadForm&id=375&ps=P. Assessed on 09 October 2012.

4   Protocol Additional to the Geneva Conventions of 12 August 1949, and relating to the Protection of Victims of Non-International Armed Conflicts (Protocol II), 8 June. http://www.icrc.org/ihl.nsf/full/475?opendocument 1977. Assessed on 09 October 2012.

5   Operations based on intelligence, planning, practise and purpose.

6   Naxal Problem Not an Armed Conflict, India tells UN. The Times of India, 18 June 2010. http://articles.timesofindia.indiatimes.com/2010-06-18/india/28276362_1_conflict-with-humanitarian-consequences-children-and-armed-conflict-radhika-coomaraswamy. Assessed on 10 October 2012.

7   A list of countries which have ratified this Protocol is available at www.icrc.org/ihl.nsf/WebSign?ReadForm&id=475&ps=P.

8   Customary international law is made up of rules that come from "a general practice accepted as law" and that exist independent of treaty law. Customary international humanitarian law (IHL) is of crucial importance in today's armed conflicts because it fills gaps left by treaty law in both international and non-international conflicts and so strengthens the protection offered to victims.

9   Jha UC. International Humanitarian Law, The Laws of War. Vij Books India.p-7.

10   Ibid. p-86. The study referred is Study on Customary International Humanitarian Law: A Contribution to the Understanding and Respect for the Rule of Law in Armed Conflict by Jean-Marie Henckaerts, available at http://www.icrc.org/eng/assets/files/other/irrc_857_henckaerts.pdf.

11   What is IHL? http://ihl.ihlresearch.org/index.cfm?fuseaction=page.

viewpage&pageid=2083. Assessed on 11 October 2012.

12   As per Additional Protocol I, military objectives are limited to those objects which by their nature, location, purpose or use make an effective contribution to military action and whose total or partial destruction, capture or neutralisation, in the circumstances ruling at the time, offers a definite military advantage. http://www.icrc.org/ihl.nsf/full/470?opendocument. Assessed on 12 October 2012.

13   Sassòli Marco. Legitimate Targets Of Attacks Under International Humanitarian Law. Background Paper, International Humanitarian Law Research Initiative. p-1. http://www.hpcrresearch.org/sites/default/files/publications/Session1.pdf. Assessed on 12 October 2012.

14   Jha.Op.cit. p—33.

15   Ibid. p-31.

16   Jha.Op.cit. p—54.

17   The full text of these rules is available on http://www.icrc.org/ihl.nsf/FULL/275?OpenDocument.

18   The Manual is available on http://ihlresearch.org/amw/HPCR%20Manual.pdf.

19   http://www.ihlresearch.org/amw/aboutmanual. Assessed on 12 October 2012.

20   Jha.Op.cit. p—54. As given by the author, these sources are: JSP 383, UK's Joint Service Manual of the Law of Armed Conflict (chapter 12 is on Air Operations) available at http://www.mod.uk/NR/rdonlyres/82702E75-9A14-4EF5-B414-49B0D7A27816/0/JSP3832004Edition.pdf, Air Force Operations and the Law (2009), published by USA's Judge Advocate General (Air), available at http://www.afjag.af.mil/shared/media/document/AFD-100510-059.pdf.

21   This definition is given in The Manual on the Law of Non- International Armed Conflict With Commentary, p-4, prepared by the International Institute of Humanitarian Law. As per the definition given in the manual, the word 'combatants' has been replaced by 'Fighters' so as to avoid any confusion with the meaning of the former term in the context of the international law of armed conflict. In this chapter, the word combatant has been used and it includes all those people actively participating in the insurgency.

22   Ibid. p- 5.

23   Ibid. p- 5.

24   HPCR Manual on International Law Applicable to Air and Missile Warfare.P-3.

25 Ibid. p-4.

26 Ibid. p-5.

27 Ibid. p-2 and 6.

28 Ibid.p-35.

29 Ibid. p-8.

30 Commentary on the HPCR Manual on International Law Applicable to Air and Missile Warfare.http://ihlresearch.org/amw/Commentary%20on%20the%20 HPCR%20Manual.pdf. Assessed on 16 October 2012.

31 Ibid.p-43.

32 This may require real time verification from various intelligence assets.

33 Ibid. p-16.Air attacks against militaryobjectives should not be allowed without using available target identification or weapon guidance technologiesto aim the weapon at those objectives when such assets are available and their use is militarilyfeasible.

34 Ibid. p-74.

35 Ibid. p-34.

36 Ibid. p- 18.

37 Ibid.p-101.Law-enforcement organisations may be incorporated into the armed forces.

38 Ibid. p-20. The opposing parties must not use the presenceor movement of the civilian population orindividual civilians to render certain points or areasimmune from air attack, in particularthey must not attempt to shield targetsfrom attacks.

39 Ibid. p- 88.

40 Ibid. p-102.

41 Ibid. p-94. If a white flag is displayed, it is a sign of surrender.

42 Article 10 of Additional Protocol I, 1977 states that in all circumstances the wounded and sick shall be treated humanely and shall receive, to the fullest extent practicable and with the least possible delay, the medical care and attention required by their condition. There shall be no distinction among them founded on any grounds other than medical ones.http://www.icrc.org/ihl.nsf/ full/470?opendocument. Assessed on 18 October 2012.

Recommendations

Requirement of a Comprehensive Strategy

The Maoist insurgency is a problem being faced by numerous states, with the threat of spreading across the entire country. As per the central government's interpretation, this insurgency is a law and order problem and is to be addressed by the affected States individually, as law and order is a State subject. The centre will assist in co-ordinating the requirement of para-military forces and other issues related to policy and governance.

Each affected State, therefore, has its own strategy of dealing with the Maoists. Some States like Andhra Pradesh have been very successful in doing so. However, what is forgotten is that the insurgents belong to the same organisation and are united in their fight against the government of the country. Their strategy in waging this insurgency is a comprehensive one and not different from State to State. What may differ are the tactics employed.

Due to the piece-meal strategy adopted by the country, if Andhra Pradesh is successful in dealing with the insurgents, the insurgents just move to adjoining States and though the insurgency may have been controlled in one State, it just increased in another State. It is akin to crossing international borders within the same country. Unified Commands have been set up in four States.[1] However, these Commands have been set up to mainly co-ordinate anti-naxal operations within the State. Though States may claim cooperation between each other,noticeable results are not visible.[2]The central government needs to take ownership of anti-naxal operations and prepare and execute a comprehensive strategy in combatting the insurgency. This strategy, not only should it holistically address socio –economic responses, but also, security related ones.

The security related response will only become effective when a co-ordinated and comprehensive strategy exists. The security operations need to be centrally planned and executed in such a manner that the insurgents are unable to take refuge from one State's police forces in another State. Accordingly, the air support provided will become more responsive and effective.

Responsive Organisational Structure, Command and Control

Air operations require centralised command and decentralised control of air assets which will always be in short supply. Centralised command ensures proper planning and utilisation of these scarce air assets by prioritisation and integration. On the other hand, decentralised execution delegates the executive authority of their utilisation to the field level, ensuring effective control, thus maximising air assets' situational responsiveness and making them tactically flexible. Maximum decentralisation of control with sufficient centralised command over the air element is what is required. As counter-insurgency operations are inherently joined, with air power playing primarily a supporting role, a high level of integration and co-ordination with the ground element is essential.

Considering that the central government takes ownership and responsibility of subduing the Maoist insurgency, a responsive organisational structure catering for centralised command and decentralised execution would be required. For ensuring such a responsive structure in a united fight against the insurgents as compared to an individual State response, the central government should appoint a Director General rank officer to head the anti-naxal operations in the country. He will be responsible for the security related response and co-ordinate with the affected States, the on-going conflict with the insurgents. Parallel to him, the post of IG Air Operations (Anti-Naxal) may be created to head the air operations in support of the counter-insurgency effort. To ensure that the ownership of these air operations remains with one civil authority (Ministry of Home Affairs), the BSF Air Wing can be designated as the air arm participating in counter-insurgency operations, with the IG Air Wing of the BSF spearheading air operations. The required personnel, expertise and equipment may be taken on deputation/loan by the BSF from the defence forces till such time that the BSF is able to create its own resources. The IG (Anti-Naxal) Operations of each affected State will be reporting to the DG (Anti-Naxal) operations. The BSF would need to position a DIG Air Operations (Anti-Naxal) in each State to co-ordinate and provide air support. These officers will report to the IG Air Operations (Anti-Naxal).

Each State can be divided into manageable geographic areas consisting of a collection of Districts. A DIG (Anti-Naxal) will head counter-insurgency operations in this area along with a DIG Air Operations (Anti-Naxal). To provide air support, each DIG Air Operations (Anti-Naxal) will command helicopter Flights deployed within ones area of responsibility. The advantages that will accrue from this organisation are:

- The insurgency which is a Pan Indian problem is addressed in an organised manner with a common strategy and goal. Each State is not left to fend for itself.

- Co-ordination between States and utilisation of resources will improve in subduing the insurgency.

- Air power expertise is available down to district level in each State.

- The local ground forces commander is able to employ air assets more effectively and to his advantage. The success of the ground operations is necessary for CI operations.

- The flexibility and employment of air assets is greatly improved.

Operational Synergy. When air power supports ground forces, the tempo of ground operations can be increased and relentlessly sustained with a lesser loss of life. Joint operations also ensure an economy of effort and resources. Towards closer integration of the air and ground forces, there will be a requirement to have sufficiently experienced and knowledgeable Air Force personnel at the headquarters directing operations, down to the lowest level. This would ensure not only joint planning but joint execution also. A model on joint operations worth emulating is the Joint Interagency Task Force. Its mission within the U.S. Southern Command Area of Responsibility is to plan, conduct, and direct interagency detection and monitoring operations of air and maritime drug smuggling activities.[3] It was established in 1994 and is composed of members from the Army, Navy, Air Force, Marine Corps, Coast Guard, and nine different law enforcement and intelligence agencies. In 2009, this Task Force was responsible for the interdiction of forty per-cent of the global cocaine trade. This proves that military and civil agencies can effectively co-ordinate and execute joint operations.

Enhancement of Air Effort. At present, 74 battalions of Central Armed Police Forces (CAPFs) and Commando Battalions for Resolute Action (CoBRA) teams Battalions are employed in anti-naxal operations.[4]The government is also planning to augment the existing CAPFs with 10,000 CRPF troops.[5]This is equivalent to more than eight army Divisions. Six IAF helicopters are presently employed for counterinsurgency operations. BSF air effort is negligible due to problems of poor serviceability of its helicopter fleet. For such a large scale mobilisation of troops, air-power resources provided for such a role are insufficient. There is an urgent need to provide more helicopters to the local police and paramilitary forces deployed against the Maoists. The BSF is in the process of acquiring six additional Mi 17 helicopters.[6] This fleet, which would augment the existing ageing fleet of Mi 17 and Dhruv helicopters, would still be insufficient for such a large scale operation. Helicopters, equipment and manpower will have to be augmented by the defence forces.

Create Infrastructure for Air Operations. Civil airfields from where air operations are mounted should be equipped with hangars. This would facilitate parking of helicopters when not in use, servicing and rectifying unserviceable helicopters. Helicopters need to be deployed as forward as possible to conserve flying hours. To increase the radius of Action, refuelling facilities at forward helipads need also to be catered for. The Indian Air Force is surveying for a new base near Bhilai in Chhattisgarh.[7] This area is strategically located in the 'Red Corridor'. At present, IAF air support is provided by the Air Commands at Nagpur and Allahabad. This base can be used for basing air assets for anti-naxal operations.[8]

Equipping and Training. Our defence forces train for conventional wars and therefore would also be equipping for such eventualities.[9] The probability of a conventional war with our adversaries is very low. Today, India's battles are being fought within its borders. In the States of J&K, Assam and its neighbouring States a 'proxy war' has been festering for a considerable period of time. The importance and requirement of involving our defence forces in protecting these Border States needs no elaboration. Another internal conflict is spreading like a red wild fire across India in the guise of the Maoist Insurgency. There are intelligence inputs confirming that the Maoists have the support of outsiders. Therefore, though a conventional war may not be fought in the future, this internal war being sponsored in whatever way by external agencies is *"encroaching India's sovereignty"*. It has to be fought and won. Hence, there is a requirement to involve our para-military forces in the best way to subdue this insurgency and assist the State police forces. For this, the government needs to equip them accordingly so that they can be trained to pacify the insurgency. This would be more applicable to the BSF Air Wing which is not fully equipped or manned to effectively take on its role of providing air support.

Troop Transportation. The importance of conducting joint air and ground operations cannot be overemphasized. The Naxalites enjoy tactical advantage in the area of operations as they have in-depth knowledge of the terrain which suits guerrilla operations. They consider roads and bridges a threat to their survival and therefore mine them extensively. These mines and IEDs have caused the maximum casualties to the security forces. Transporting troops by air will neutralise the Maoist tactic of mining roads. The Maoists are alive to the threat they face from the air. They have trained their cadres in facets of Air Defence. Sanitizing landing areas by using armed helicopters will practically ensure no loss of helicopters to ground fire during the take-off and landing phases and while disembarking troops. This option should be kept open.

Enhancing Surveillance and Reconnaissance Air Effort. It is an accepted fact that intelligence is essential in fighting any insurgency. It is also known that the security forces are bereft of intelligence. There is no doubt that ground level intelligence obtained from

HUMINT is necessary in subduing the Maoists. However, aerial surveillance and reconnaissance can give a great amount of data. Aerial surveillance using UAVs needs to be enhanced. More UAVs need to be inducted to provide continuous surveillance and assist in building a comprehensive intelligence picture. The advantage of such surveillance has already been brought out in detail. Other than using MALE UAVs (medium altitude long endurance) which can operate up to 30,000 feet altitude and have a range of over 200 km, micro UAVs which are launched by the hand also need to be inducted.[10]

Aerial imagery requires analysing and interpreting. Therefore, when aerial surveillance is enhanced, there would also be a requirement of increasing the availability of Photo Interpreters (PIs) and associated infrastructure to produce actionable intelligence. Intelligence is time sensitive. Demand and supply procedures between the field forces and intelligence agencies should be streamlined and practised.

In addition to being able to obtain intelligence through aerial video surveillance, technology has made it possible to track moving humans concealed under vegetation and buried objects such as mines and IEDs.[11] India must invest in obtaining such equipment and using it in locating IEDs and mines which are responsible for the heavy casualty toll suffered by the security forces.

Casualty Evacuation. The CRPF and other police forces are engaged in an asymmetric battle against the Maoist insurgents. The battle fields are the jungles of central India and remote areas. Injured security forces, if evacuated to medical facilities by surface transport, will have to travel considerable distances and at times their condition may deteriorate. They deserve a fighting chance to survive injuries sustained in a fight for preserving the integrity of the Nation. Ensuring that injured troops receive medical aid and a chance to survive is a moral obligation on the part of the government. Towards this, sufficient air effort has to be made available for CASEVAC. All major operations should be supported from the air. At least one helicopter should be earmarked on ground standby to evacuate any casualty during minor operations. A dedicated fleet of medical helicopters for this purpose needs to be created.

Psychological Air Operations. PSYOP messages distributed from the air extolling the Maoists the advantages of laying down their arms and returning to main stream life should be practised. Offensive air power when used indiscriminately can result in losing the support of the people and escalating the insurgency. However, when offensive air operations are prudently planned, the demoralising psychological aspects of such operations on the Maoists must be factored in and reinforced by PSYOP messages.

Supporting Civil Administration. The government needs to increase its visibility and make its presence felt in insurgency affected areas, which would bring in better governance and in turn facilitate winning back the support of the people. Such areas are generally plagued with poor road connectivity and the normal civil servant would hesitate in moving out to administer these areas due to reasons of personal safety. Civil helicopters can be employed to transport the entire gamut of civil administrative machinery (including food and medical aid) to remote areas.

Role of Media. Public opinion plays a very important role in influencing government action against the insurgents. In December 1856, Abraham Lincoln, in a speech, bringing out the importance of public opinion said, "*Our government rests in public opinion. Whoever can change public opinion can change the government*".[12] In the world of today which is overloaded with various media channels, media has a great persuasive value. It can influence public opinion and perception regarding any issue – depending on how the issue is projected by the media.

The centre of gravity in any insurgency is the people. The insurgents will try and win over the population with their ideology, while the government has to win back the support of this population. Public perception on how the government is fighting the insurgents and not using excessive force, brutality or incorrect methods is vital to the success of this campaign.

The media, which is known to be very responsible in reporting matters of national security, has to be taken into confidence and explained the requirements and advantages of using airpower in all its roles. If air power is to be used against the insurgents, public opinion has to be moulded about how air power is supporting the ground forces and ensure that it is assisting in reducing the casualty rate of the ground forces and ensure that they suffer minimum casualties and hardships. If and when air power is used in the offensive role, the government has to be able to justify the restraint in its use and emphasise on the strict rules of engagement being followed to ensure minimal collateral damage. It has to justify and legitimise the use of airpower to the public. What better way than the media can be used to do so?

Today, the penetration of media has reached all strata of society. During the Telangana struggle, only one paper was available to 111 people. Newspaper circulations increased to 60 people to a newspaper during the Naxalite movement. At the height of the terror spread in Punjab in 1984, television was controlled by the government.[13] Today, according to a report published by the Internet and Mobile Association of India, there are 38 million internet users in rural India.[14] Television viewership has grown from 120 million in 2007 to 148 million in 2012.[15] As per the 55th Annual Report of Registrar of Newspapers for India (RNI) for 2010-11 titled "Press in India", the total circulation of newspapers stood at 32,92,04,841, with 82,237 newspapers registered in India.[16] Information is available to one and all today. Therefore, the media with its high levels of following and ability to influence the minds of people plays an important role in moulding public opinion. The government must make the most of this readily available platform.

Concluding Observations

Any counterinsurgency campaign has to be based on a strong political will, aggressive anti-guerrilla tactics and economic and social development of affected areas to win back the confidence of the people. To ensure development of these areas, the lack of which was the root cause for the people taking to arms, a pre-requisite is to regain control of insurgency affected areas.This is ensured by the security forces.In conducting counterinsurgency operations, the ground force is the primary force responsible for ensuring security.

Airpower is normally not employed as it is synonymous to destructive fire power and traditionally considered to be best utilised when fighting a foreign enemy and not citizens of the country. Its utilisation also attracts tremendous public attention. However, when counterinsurgency operations are integrated with the support roles of airpower, the insurgency can be defeated in a shorter period with less loss of life and resources.The use of airpower provides the option of observing the movements and locating insurgent locations from the air, flying in reinforcements and delivering fire support as necessary.Evacuation of injured personnel by air from the field directly to medical aid is an important role which has a positive effect of boosting troop morale. The major contribution of air power in combating insurgencies is restricting the use of conventional options by the insurgents, improving the response time of the security forces, and enabling security forces to seize tactical initiative.

The Government of India has permitted the employment of airpower. There are some lacunas in its employment which when addressed, would put the Naxalites on a back foot.Counter-insurgency operations need to be joint, with air power playing primarily a supporting role. Therefore, a high level of integration and co-ordination with the ground element is essential. To be effective, the quantum of flying effort needs to commensurate with the requirement and be sufficiently supported with infrastructure. It must be borne in mind that the distinctive characteristics of air power — speed, ability to overcome physical barriers, range, flexibility, and psychological effect — makes it essential to counterinsurgency operations.

Endnotes

1   A Unified Command has been set up in each of the States of Chhattisgarh, West Bengal, Jharkhand and Orissa. The Unified Command are to have officers from the security establishment, besides civilian officers representing the civil administration and it will carry out carefully planned anti-naxal operations. The command & control setup in these States have been re-structured and an IG from CRPF posted in each of these States is to work in close co-ordination with IG (anti-naxal operation) in the State. Ministry of Home Affairs, Annual Report 2010-11. p-25. mha.nic.in/pdfs/AR(E)1011.pdf. Assessed on 19

November 2012.

2   Left Wing Extremism. Report prepared by CLAWS. p-137.

3   Joint Interagency Task Force. http://www.globalsecurity.org/military/agency/
     dod/jitf.htm. Assessed on 06 March 2012.Munsing Evan and Lamb Christopher.
     Joint Interagency Task Force.Strategic Perspective -5. Institute for National
     Strategic Studies. p-3. http://www.ndu.edu/inss/docuploaded/Strat%20
     Perspectives%205%20_%20Lamb-Munsing.pdf. Assessed on 06 March 2012.

4   Ministry of Home Affairs, Annual Report 2011-12. p-34. http://mha.nic.in/
     pdfs/AR(E)1112.pdf. Assessed on 19 November 2012.

5   Anti-naxal ops: Govt to deploy 10,000 CRPF troopers Press Trust of India /
     New Delhi October 31, 2012. http://www.business-standard.com/generalnews/
     news/anti-naxal-ops-govt-to-deploy-10000-crpf-troopers/74289/. Assessed on
     19 November 2012.

6   The Ministry of Home Affairs (MHA) is purchasing helicopters from Russia to
     support anti-Naxal operations. The Indian Air Force has been asked to buy an
     additional six Mi-17 V5 helicopters for the BSF from Russia, with which the
     latter is negotiating a follow on order of 59 helicopters. http://newindianexpress.
     com/nation/article316373. Assessed on 21 November 2012.

7   The Push into Naxal Territory.Tehelka Magazine, Vol 7, Issue 28, Dated July
     17, 2010. http://tehelka.com/story_main46.asp?filename=Ne170710naxalter
     ritory.asp. Assessed on 06 September 2012.

8   Ibid.

9   As per an internet article, during an interview by Nitin A. Gokhale, the
     Security and Strategic Affairs Editor NDTV, the then Chief of Air Staff, Air
     Chief Marshal PV Naik said, "Armed forces, army navy and air force, in my
     opinion should not be used for internal security at all. Our training is different.
     We train in lethal action. We train in destruction of an adversary across the
     border who is trying to encroach into India's sovereignty." http://nitinagokhale.
     blogspot.in/2012/07/why-air-force-is-wary-of-role-in-anti.html. Assessed on
     05 September 2012.

10   The IAF, for instance, has issued an RFI (request for information) to armament
     companies for micro UAVs with an "operational endurance in excess of 30
     minutes" but weighing less than two kg to ensure they can even be operated
     by a single person. The Army is in the process of inducting slightly bigger
     mini and micro spy drones in a major way for short-range surveillance and
     intelligence-gathering missions. RajatPanditSpy in the sky: India begins hunt
     for mini 'killer' drones . The Times of India, 02 Augast 2012. http://articles.

timesofindia.indiatimes.com/2010-08-02/india/28274524_1_spy-drones-ucavs-unmanned-combat-aerial-vehicles. Assessed on 26 November 2012.

11   The Carabas VHF synthetic aperture radar developed by Saab Microwave Systems is one such system.This synthetic aperature radar was to be ready for field evaluation and trials in early 2010 using evaluation kits for mounting on light helicopters. This system can also be mounted on an UAV.http://www.saabgroup.com/Templates/Public/Pages/PrintAllTabs.aspx?pageId=1448. Assessed on 26 November 2012.

12   Lincoln Abraham.Writings of Abraham Lincoln, Volume 2.http://www.classicreader.com/book/3331/96/. Assessed on 22 November 2012.

13   More thanMaoism, edited by Jeffrey Robin, SenRonjoy and Singh Pratima. Manohar Publications. Refer to Jeffery Robin. Media and Maoism, p-341-342.

14   Internet in Rural India 2012.Published by Internet and Mobile Association of India. p- 4. http://www.iamai.in/Upload/Research/9320123264601/ICube_2012_Rural_Internet_Final_62.pdf. Assessed on 22 November 2012.

15   Vinod Kumar Menon. Is this the end of cable mafia? http://www.mid-day.com/news/2012/jan/170112-Is-this-the-end-of-cable-mafia.htm. Assessed on 22 November 2012.

16   Press Information Bureau, Government of India. http://pib.nic.in/newsite/erelease.aspx?relid=79265. Assessed on 22 November 2012.

ORGANISATION CHART

PEOPLES LIBERATION GUERRILLA ARMY

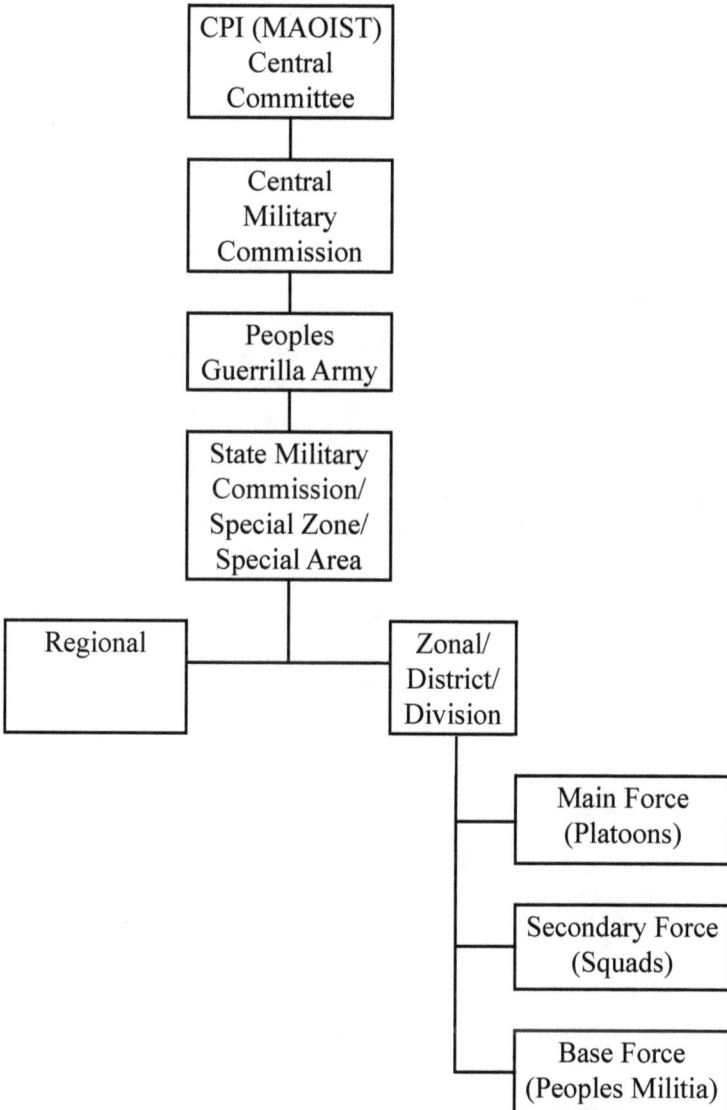

www.ingramcontent.com/pod-product-compliance
Lightning Source LLC
Chambersburg PA
CBHW070155310326
41914CB00100B/1935/J